C000282733

GREENWOOD
GUIDES

The Team

Fiona Greenwood

Simon Greenwood

Adam Barnes

Guy Mavor

First published in 2000 by Greenwood Guides,
10 Oliphant St, London W10 4EG, UK.

Second edition

Copyright © August 2002 Greenwood Guides

All rights reserved. No part of this publication may be reproduced, or
transmitted in any form or by any means, electronically or mechanically,
including photocopying, recording or any information storage or retrieval system
without prior written permission from the publisher. This publication is not
included under licences issued by the Copyright Agency. No part of this
publication may be used in any form of advertising, sales promotion or publicity.

Simon Greenwood has asserted his right to be identified as the author of this
work.

ISBN 0-9537980-2-X printed in China.

THE GREENWOOD GUIDE TO
SOUTH AFRICA
special hand-picked accommodation

**Including Phophonyane Lodge in Swaziland
and Malealea Lodge in Lesotho**

Second Edition

www.greenwoodguides.com

Acknowledgements

I would like to extend our particular thanks to Mike and Jackie Solomon. They provided a real home for us all in Riebeek West, cooked us countless meals, and generally made sure that we lived at a level far higher than we are either used to or deserve. See Tigertrap Cottages, book number 35. Our thanks also to Adam and Guy for being thrown in the deep end and swimming off like dolphins!

Editorship, administration and production Simon and Fiona Greenwood

Writing collaboration and inspections Simon and Fiona Greenwood, Adam Barnes and Guy Mavor. Much is still owed to Sam Harris for all the research and writing he did for the first edition.

Cover artwork Patricia Fraser

Maps created by InformAge, GIS, using ESRI's Arcview™, from digital topographic and road data sourced from the South African Directorate: Surveys and Mapping

Typesetting, conversion and reprographics Avonset, Bath, UK

Printing, Colorcraft, Hong Kong

UK Distribution, Portfolio, London

SA Distribution, Quartet Sales and Marketing, Johannesburg

Incidental photographs

Title page: Wildebeest, Isibindi Lodge

Province intro pages

Limpopo, Cheetah, Lion Sands Private Game Reserve

Western Cape, Dolphin Jump, Whale and Dolphin Centre, Plettenberg Bay

Eastern Cape, Giraffe, Lion Sands Private Game Reserve

KwaZulu Natal, Leopard, Lion Sands Private Game Reserve

Mpumalanga, Lion, Lion Sands Private Game Reserve

North West, Impala and Oxpecker, Lion Sands Private Game Reserve

Northern Cape, Lion Sands Private Game Reserve

Gauteng, Trevor Thompson, Seaforth Farm

Free State, Lesotho, Klipspringer by Andries Barnard

Swaziland, Lilac-breasted Roller by Helen Barnard

Symbols
and what they mean

 No credit cards accepted

 Meals can be provided, often by prior arrangement

 Rooms all have TVs

 Stocked wild game can be seen. This does not include naturally occurring wild animals like springbok and waterbuck

 Children are welcome without proviso

 Working farm

 Off-street car parking

 Access only for wheelchairs

 Full wheelchair facilities

 Swimming available in pool, sea, dam or river

 Good hiking or walking direct from the house

 They have their own horses for riding

Contents

Introduction

Those that have already fallen, by design or serendipity, into the Greenwood Guides' clutches will know by now something of our motivations. If I start repeating myself give me a nudge, or raise your hand and ask to be excused.

Our aim with this guide book is to help you get the most out of your holiday to South Africa.

To this end we have driven the length and breadth of the land, staying in guest houses, B&Bs, farms, game lodges and self-catering cottages. We have checked them out for you, tasted the wines, eaten the dinners, the breakfasts, drunk the cups of tea, the coffees, the wines; evaluated the game drives, bumped off down farm tracks to see the private gorge or mountain, tasted the wines…look, it's been tough ok! Actually it is not all fun and games, in case you're printing off your CV… although most of it is. You would not wish to follow us to many of the places we visit. And, hardest of all, we have had to turn down OK places that did not excite quite enough.

We hope, as a result of this culling process, that you will learn to trust the guide and the descriptions. The more that you trust it the more useful it will become. We hope that you will feel more willing to drive down a long dirt road to a secluded farm if you know that we have already been there before you and given it the thumbs up.

At its simplest the Greenwood Guides approach is to recommend places that we have been to ourselves and particularly liked. Some of you might want to know what exactly it is that we DO like… which is fair enough.

Read on.

EXPENSIVE DOES NOT MEAN GOOD

There are many publications offering collections of places to stay. Each has its own approach but none, it seems, has considered what actually-really-truly represents a great place to stay. Places are usually gathered at a similar price level and sold to a 'market' in that perceived income bracket: budget, upmarket, etc.

But expensive does not necessarily mean good. Nor does cheap, however appealing the word may sound! If a place costs plenty then it will probably offer facilities in keeping with the price. But that does not mean you will have any fun. Some very expensive places forget that they are providing a service and look down their noses at their own guests. At the other end of the spectrum, the very cheapest places are often cheap for good reasons. Sometimes for really tremendous reasons!

Luxury, of course, varies with price… but people and character don't. Charm and genuine, friendly hospitality, the extra qualities we search for, are found spaced evenly across the price spectrum. The places to stay in this guide range from R150 – R3000 per person per night. Nowhere cuts corners at the risk of your displeasure! We give equal billing to each place we choose, no matter if it is a gorgeous game lodge or a home-spun B&B.

At the top end, the most jewel-encrusted, bijou, nay 'boutique' places may drip with luxurious trimmings, but are still, in almost all cases, family-owned and -run and all have retained their sense of atmosphere and humour and are friendly and informal.

Equally there are places in the book hidden in secret valleys or up mountains, without electricity, but with gas-heated free-standing baths, verandahs hung with hurricane lamps or candles, wonderful views and charming hosts.

It is the quality of experience that draws us in and this is not determined by how much you pay.

GO WEST! GO EAST!

We take you, by preference, off the beaten track and away from the ever-deepening furrows ploughed by mass tourism… not hard to do as tourism is a youthful 'industry' in South Africa (in effect it started in 1994). The first waves of visitors have tended to visit a limited amount of the country – the Garden Route, Hermanus, Franschhoek, the Kruger National Park, Cape Town, Oudtshoorn. As time goes on more travellers will be found in the company of those Eastern Cape farmers hidden away in their idyllic valleys. Or tramping the craggy gardens of the Cederberg. Or just picking a place from the book that they like the look of rather than trying to match their accommodation to the 'icons of tourism' pushed at them back in Britain or wherever. Many of the places in the book are far more exciting destinations in themselves and you won't have to share.

In the end I know that you will really like the owners in this book, many of whom we now count as friends. And you will certainly make friends yourselves if you stick to the Greenwood trail. I know, I know… I would say that! You'll just have to try it out for yourself.

Wherever you plump for, you will be welcomed with genuine warmth. South Africans are like that. And it is a fact that is constantly commented on by first-time visitors….

… from whom we hear a great deal. Many arrive with preconceived notions, based, I suppose, on the apartheid years, and negative press reporting on the bigger (and undeniable) social ills. They have commented in unison (and often with surprise) on the extraordinary value for money, the reliably warm and natural hospitality, the high standards of food and wine, the amazing variety of things to do, scenery to experience and people to meet. This is a country going through a fascinating period of change and there is an uplifting and dynamic sense of history taking place beneath your feet.

We concentrate solely on accommodation in this guide, preferring to allow the owners in the book to advise, with far more up-to-date expertise, on where to eat and what to do when you get there. But nonetheless here are some tips and recommendations that I suggest you read in case you find them helpful.

DRIVING
There is nowhere in this book that would make a 4-wheel drive a necessity.

CAR HIRE
Make sure that you have considered the amount of daily mileage your car hire company gives you. 100 km or even 200 km a day is virtually nothing and the final cost can be far higher than you estimated. Try and work out roughly what distances you will be covering and ask for the correct daily allowance.

MOBILE/CELL PHONES
Airports all have shops that provide mobile phones. They are invaluable and we recommend that you get one. You can buy a cheap handset and then pay for calls as you go with recharge cards. You don't need to get locked into year-long contracts.

TELEPHONE NUMBERS

To call South Africa from the UK dial 0027 then drop the 0 from the local code.

To call the UK from South Africa dial 0944 the drop the 0 from the local code.

The numbers printed in this book are all from within South Africa.

TORTOISES

Look out for tortoises. They are slow, but seem to spend a lot of time, completely against accepted tortoise wisdom, crossing roads.

TIPPING

* In restaurants we tend to give 15%. This seems fair to me as many overseas currencies make things really very cheap in South Africa and there is no two-tier system in place to make things easier for South Africans earning the rand.

* At a petrol station my policy is to give no tip for just filling up, 3 rand for cleaning the windows, and 5 rand for cleaning the windows and checking oil and water. If you really don't want the attendant to clean your windows you need to make this a statement when you ask for the petrol… or they will often do it anyway.

* At a guest house I would typically give R15 per person staying for up to two nights. If you are staying longer than two nights then you might feel like adding more. If there is obviously one maid to whom the tip will go then give it to her direct. If there are many staff members who will be sharing the tip then give it to your host.

TIME OF YEAR

I got in a bit of a tangle in the first edition trying neatly to package up what is really very complicated. So I will limit myself to one observation. It seems to me that most Europeans come to South Africa in January, February and March to avoid their own miserable weather and write taunting postcards home from a sunny Cape. I've been doing this myself for the last few years.

However, the very best time of year to visit the Northern Cape, Mpumalanga, Northern Province (Limpopo as it is now nicely to be known), North-West Province, KwaZulu Natal and the Karoo, i.e. the whole country except the southern Cape, is from May to October. The air is dry and warm, game viewing is at its best and there are fewer tourists keeping the prices higher. It's worth mentioning.

PAY FOR ENTRY

We could not afford to research and publish this guide in the way we do without the financial support of those we feature. Each place that we have chosen has paid an entry fee for which we make no apology. It has not influenced our decision-making about who is right or wrong for the guide and we turn down many more than we accept. The proof of this is in the proverbial pudding. Use the book and see for yourself. It is also very hard for us to write up a place that we are not enthusiastic about.

THE MAPS SECTION

The maps at the front of the book are designed to show you where in the country each place is positioned, and should not be used as a road map. There are many minor and dirt roads missing and we recommend that you buy a proper companion road atlas.

Each place is flagged with a number that corresponds to the page number below each entry.

Some have complained that it is hard to find detailed road maps of South Africa in the UK, so I suggest you buy one at the airport when you arrive in SA.

CANCELLATION

Most places have some form of cancellation charge. Do make sure that you are aware what this is if you book in advance. Owners need to protect themselves against no-shows and will often demand a deposit for advance booking.

PRICES

The prices quoted are per person sharing per night, unless specifically stated otherwise. Every now and then complications have meant we quote the full room rate. Single rates are also given.

We have usually put in a range within which the actual price will fall. This may be because of fluctuating prices at different times of year, but also we have tried to predict the anticipated rise in prices over the book's shelf life. Obviously we cannot know what will happen to the value of the rand over such a long period of time and prices might fall outside the quoted range.

Most game lodges quote an all-in package including meals and game activities.

CHILDREN

We have only given the child-friendly symbol to those places that are unconditionally accepting of the little fellows. This does not necessarily mean that if there is no symbol children are barred. But it may mean chatting with your hosts about their ages, their temperaments and how suitable a time and place it will be. Most owners are concerned about how their other guests will take to kids running wild when they are trying to relax on a long-anticipated holiday… from their own children.

RIDING

We have only given this symbol to places with their own horses. Many places can organise riding nearby.

DISCLAIMER

We make no claims to god-like objectivity in assessing what is or is not special about the places we feature. They are there because we like them. Our opinions and tastes are mortal and ours alone. We have done our utmost to get the facts right, but apologize for any mistakes that may have slipped through the net. Some things change which are outside our control: people sell up, prices increase, exchange rates fluctuate, unfortunate extensions are added, marriages break up and even acts of God can rain down destruction. We would be grateful to be told about any errors or changes, however great or small. We can always make these editions on the web version of this book.

DON'T TRY AND DO TOO MUCH. PLEASE.

It is the most common way to spoil your own holiday. South Africa is a huge country and you cannot expect to see too much of it on one trip. Don't over-extend yourself. Stay everywhere for at least two nights and make sure that you aren't spending your hard-earned holiday fiddling with the radio and admiring the dashboard of your hire car.

PLEASE WRITE TO US

Our email address is editor@greenwoodguides.com for all comments. We are always grateful to hear how much/little you enjoyed the places in the book.

We also have a guide to Australia and New Zealand and should, if all goes according to plan, have our first Canadian guide ready by January 2003. These books are available in bookshops or by emailing us direct.

FOR TAILOR-MADE TOURS

If you are interested in a tailor-made tour using the places to stay in this book, we recommend two operators, both working from within South Africa:

Tripos Tours, run by Lyndon Burt, operates primarily in South Africa, but also puts together tours to Namibia, Botswana and the Indian Ocean Islands (particularly Bazaruto in Mozambique). Specialist areas include scheduled tours to Tuli, Chobe and Victoria Falls, as well as private lettings in the Western Cape. Tripos is IATA licensed and can take care of all the air and land arrangements of a tour of Greenwood properties. Contact details: tripos@icon.co.za, www.tripostravel.co.za, tel: 021-689-8962, fax: 021-689-6821.

Parker Tours, run by Jim Parker (also the owner of Old Rearsby Farm Cottages, book number 144), pioneered the first in-bound scheduled and quoted tours to South Africa with flexible options on demand. Contact details: tours@parkertours.co.za, tel: 033-263-2280 or 033-263-1331.

A WORD ABOUT WEBSITES

Some website addresses in this book may feature additional places that we have not necessarily visited and therefore cannot recommend.

THE CAPE SALMON

In the last edition I suggested that the Cape salmon is not a salmon at all. I have since been told that in fact it *is* a salmon after all. The debate continues....

General Map

Approximate scale 1 : 9.2 million

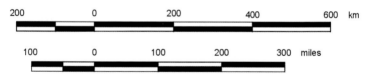

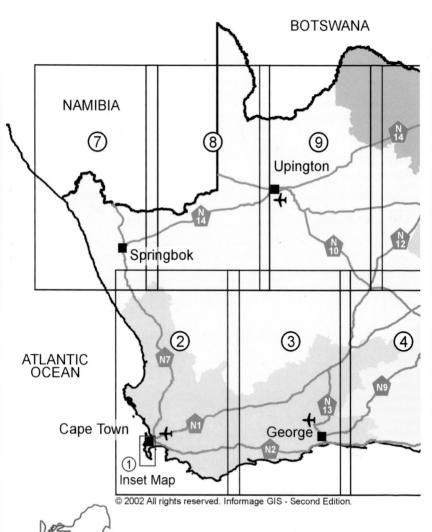

BOTSWANA

NAMIBIA

⑦

⑧

⑨

Upington

N14

N14

Springbok

N10

N12

ATLANTIC
OCEAN

②

③

④

N7

N9

N1

N13

Cape Town

George

N2

① Inset Map

© 2002 All rights reserved. Informage GIS - Second Edition.

The size of Britain
in relation to South Africa

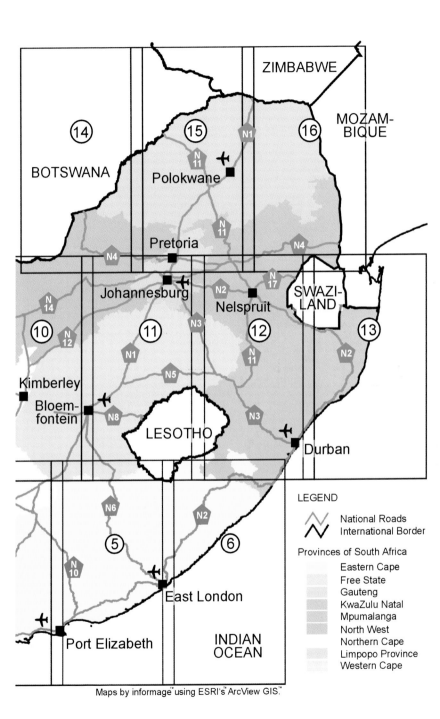

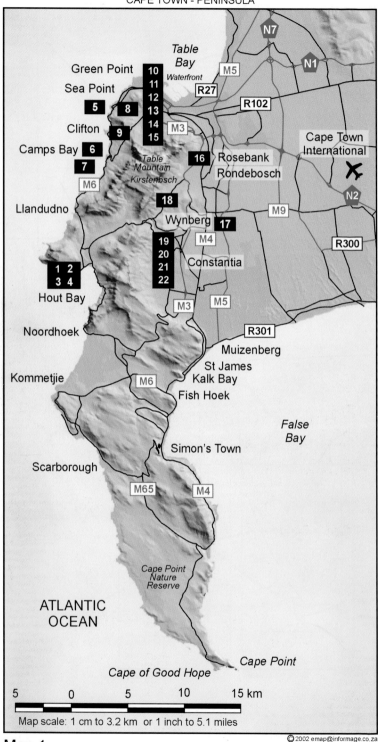

CAPE TOWN - PENINSULA

Table Bay

Green Point

Waterfront

Sea Point

Clifton

Camps Bay

Llandudno

Table Mountain Kirstenbsch

Rosebank

Rondebosch

Cape Town International

Wynberg

Constantia

Hout Bay

Noordhoek

Muizenberg

St James

Kalk Bay

Fish Hoek

Kommetjie

False Bay

Scarborough

Simon's Town

Cape Point Nature Reserve

ATLANTIC OCEAN

Cape of Good Hope

Cape Point

5   0   5   10   15 km

Map scale: 1 cm to 3.2 km   or 1 inch to 5.1 miles

Map 1

© 2002 emap@informage.co.za

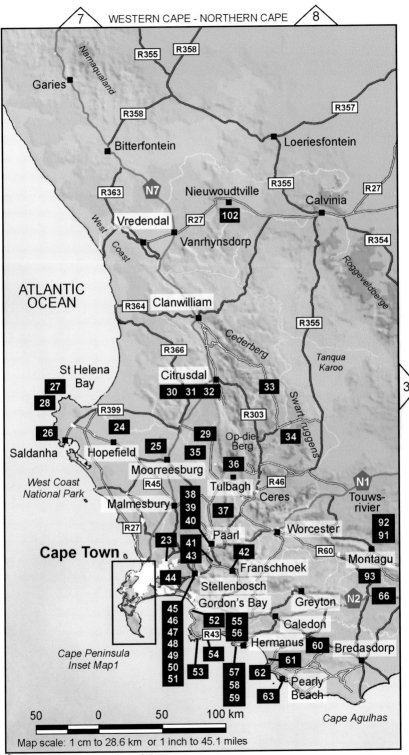

© 2002 All rights reserved informage GIS emap@informage.co.za

Map scale: 1 cm to 28.6 km or 1 inch to 45.1 miles

Map 2

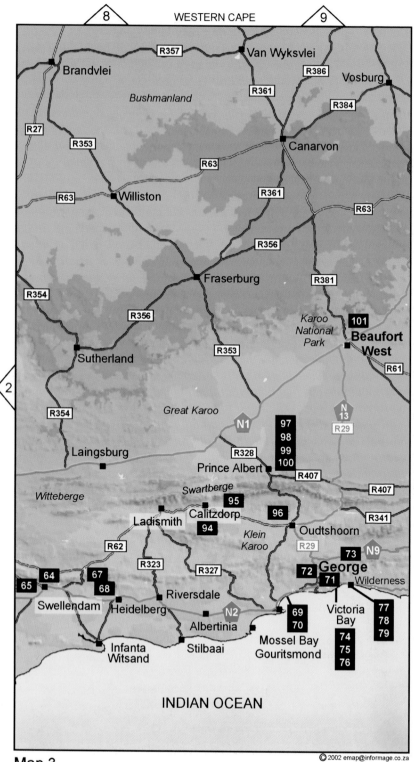

8

9

R357

Brandvlei

Bushmanland

Van Wyksvlei

R386

R361

Vosburg

R384

R27

R353

Canarvon

R63

R63

Williston

R361

R63

R356

2

R354

Fraserburg

R356

R381

Karoo National Park

101

Beaufort West

Sutherland

R353

R61

R354

Great Karoo

N1

97
98
99
100

N13

R29

Laingsburg

R328

Prince Albert

R407

R407

Swartberge

95

96

R341

Witteberge

Ladismith

Calitzdorp

94

Klein Karoo

Oudtshoorn

R29

R62

R323

R327

73

N9

72 **George**

71

Wilderness

Riversdale

64

67
68

65

N2

69
70

Victoria Bay

77
78
79

Swellendam

Heidelberg

Albertinia

Mossel Bay
Gouritsmond

74
75
76

Infanta
Witsand

Stilbaai

INDIAN OCEAN

Map 3

© 2002 emap@informage.co.za

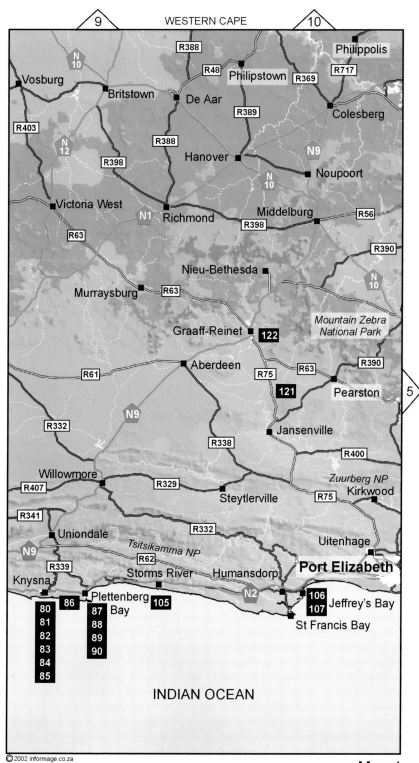

WESTERN CAPE

Philippolis
R717
Vosburg
R388
R48
Philipstown
R369
N10
Britstown
De Aar
Colesberg
R389
R403
R388
Hanover
N9
Noupoort
R398
N10
Victoria West
N1
Richmond
Middelburg
R56
R398
R63
R390
Nieu-Bethesda
N10
Murraysburg
R63
Graaff-Reinet
122
Mountain Zebra National Park
R61
Aberdeen
R63
R390
R75
121
R332
N9
Pearston
5
R338
Jansenville
R400
Willowmore
R329
R407
Steytlerville
Zuurberg NP
R75
Kirkwood
R341
N9
Uniondale
R332
Uitenhage
R339
Tsitsikamma NP
R62
Port Elizabeth
Knysna
86
Storms River
Humansdorp
N2
106
107
80
81
82
83
84
85
87
88
89
90
Plettenberg Bay
105
Jeffrey's Bay
St Francis Bay

INDIAN OCEAN

© 2002 informage.co.za

Map 4

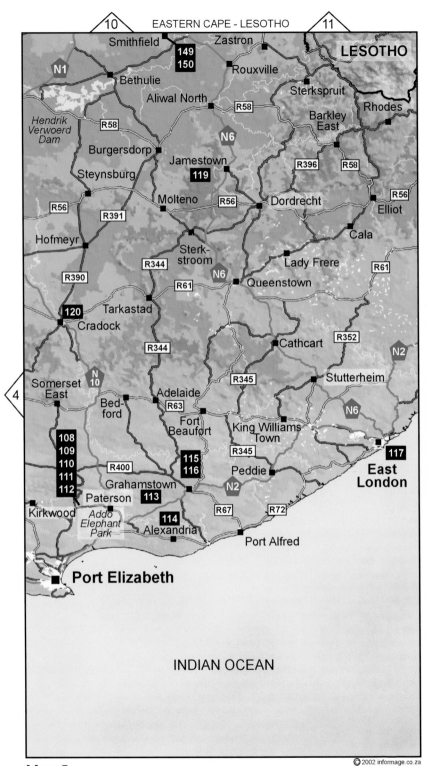

Map 5

© 2002 informage.co.za

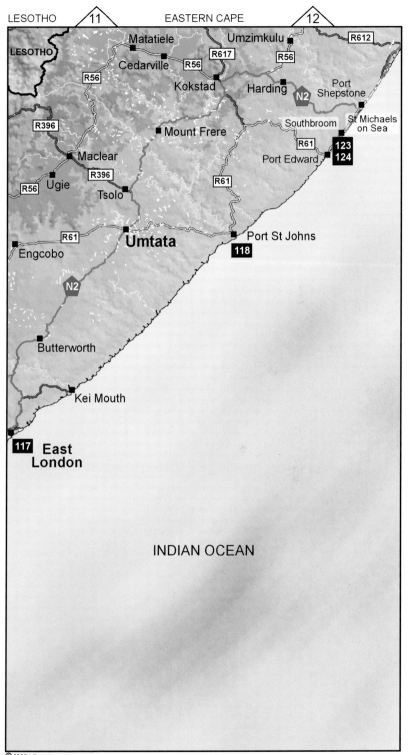

LESOTHO

Matatiele

Cedarville

R56

R56

R617

Umzimkulu

R56

R612

Kokstad

Harding

N2

Port Shepstone

R396

Southbroom

St Michaels on Sea

Mount Frere

R61

123
124

Port Edward

Maclear

R396

Ugie

R56

Tsolo

R61

R61

Engcobo

Umtata

Port St Johns

118

N2

Butterworth

Kei Mouth

117 East London

INDIAN OCEAN

© 2002 informage.co.za

Map 6

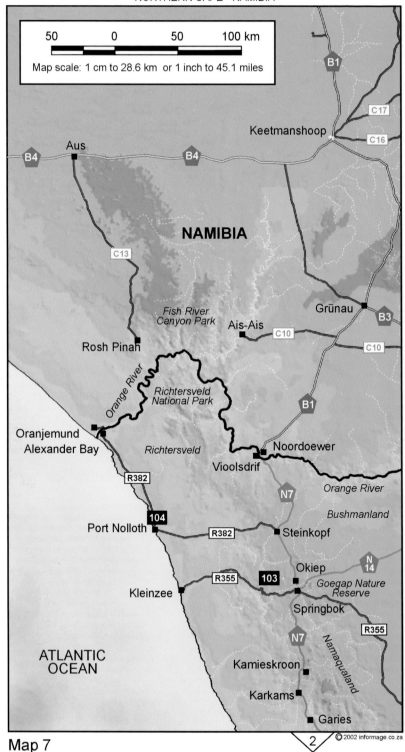

50   0   50   100 km

Map scale: 1 cm to 28.6 km or 1 inch to 45.1 miles

B1

C17

Keetmanshoop

C16

Aus

B4   B4

NAMIBIA

C13

*Fish River
Canyon Park*   Ais-Ais   C10   Grünau   B3

Rosh Pinah   C10

Orange River   *Richtersveld
National Park*   B1

Oranjemund
Alexander Bay   *Richtersveld*   Noordoewer

Vioolsdrif   *Orange River*

R382   N7   *Bushmanland*

104   *Steinkopf*

Port Nolloth   R382   N
14

Okiep   *Goegap Nature
Reserve*

R355   103

Kleinzee   Springbok

ATLANTIC
OCEAN   N7   *Namaqualand*   R355

Kamieskroon

Karkams

Garies

Map 7   2   © 2002 informage.co.za

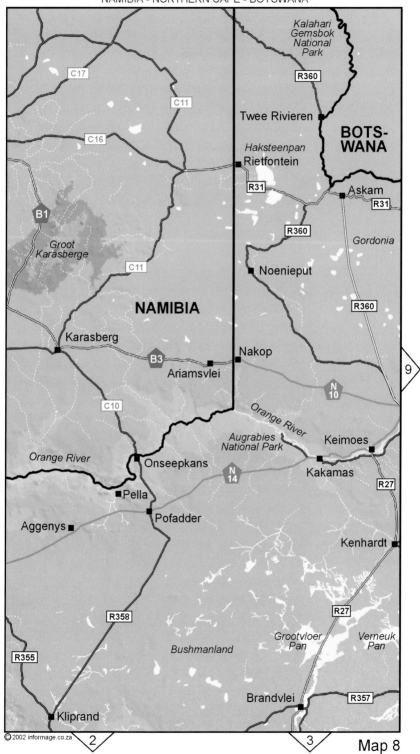

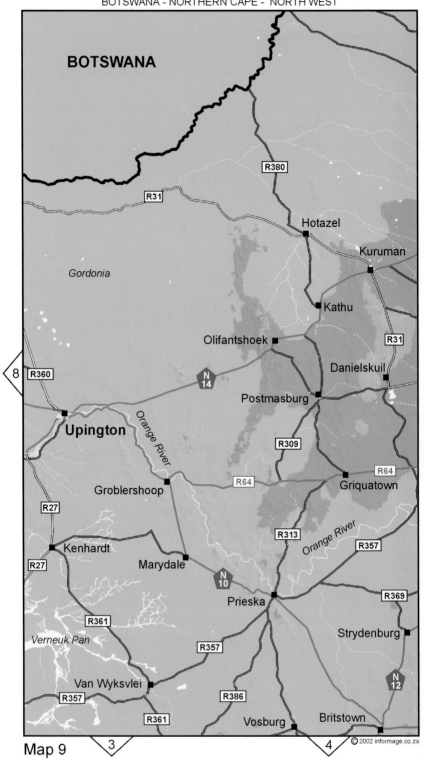

Map 9

© 2002 informage.co.za

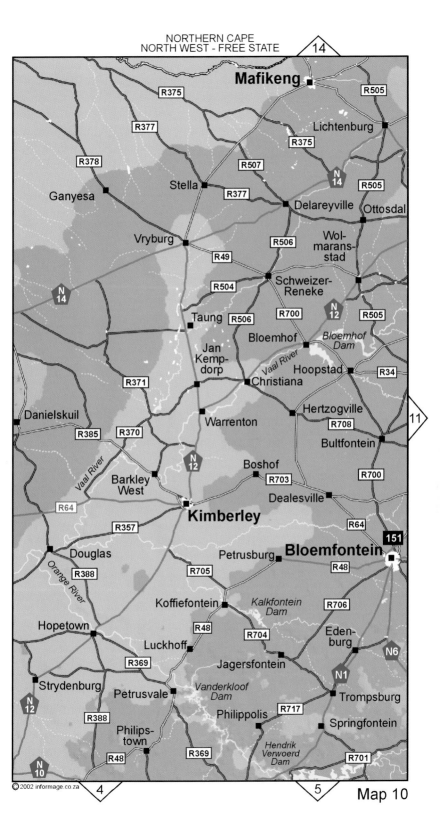

Mafikeng

R505

R375

Lichtenburg

R377

R375

R378

R507

N14

R505

Ganyesa

Stella

R377

Delareyville

Ottosdal

Vryburg

R506

Wol-
marans-
stad

R49

Schweizer-
Reneke

R504

Taung

R506

R700

N12

R505

Bloemhof

*Bloemhof
Dam*

Jan
Kemp-
dorp

Vaal River

Hoopstad

R34

R371

Christiana

Warrenton

Hertzogville

R708

Bultfontein

11

Danielskuil

R385

R370

Vaal River

N12

Boshof

R703

R700

Barkley
West

Dealesville

R64

Kimberley

R64

151

R357

Bloemfontein

Douglas

Petrusburg

R48

R388

R705

Koffiefontein

*Kalkfontein
Dam*

R706

Hopetown

R48

Eden-
burg

N6

Luckhoff

R704

Jagersfontein

N1

R369

Strydenburg

Petrusvale

*Vanderkloof
Dam*

Trompsburg

N12

R388

Philippolis

R717

Springfontein

Philips-
town

R48

R369

*Hendrik
Verwoerd
Dam*

R701

N10

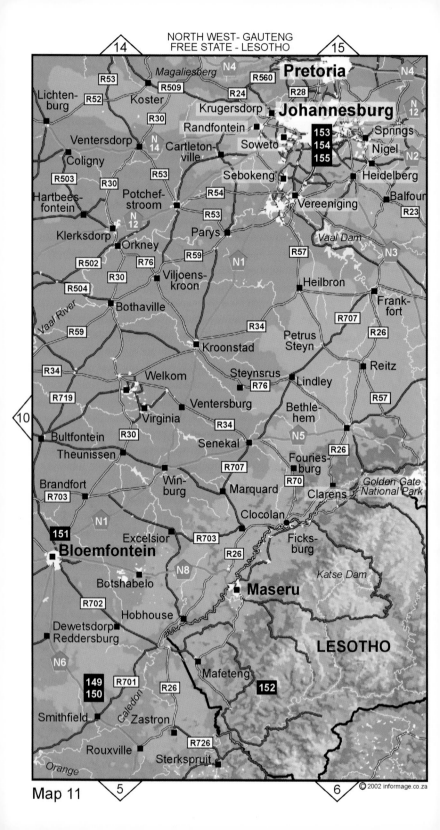

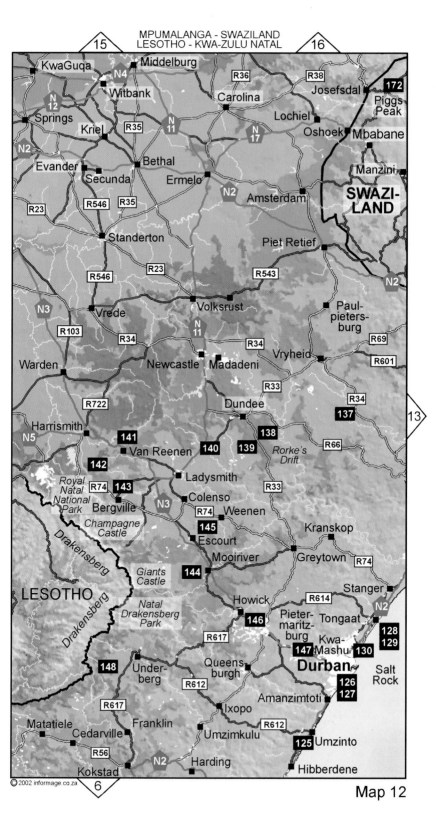

Map 12

© 2002 informage.co.za

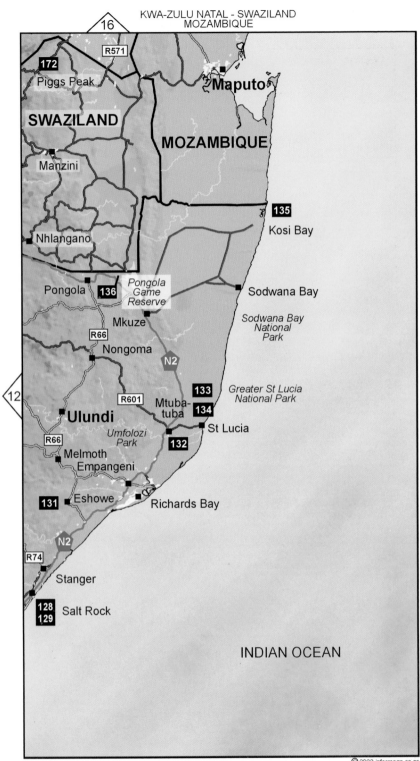

Map 13

© 2002 informage.co.za

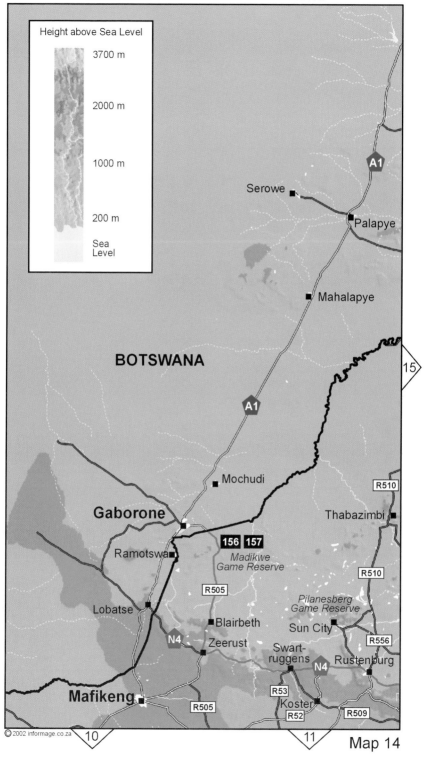

Map 14

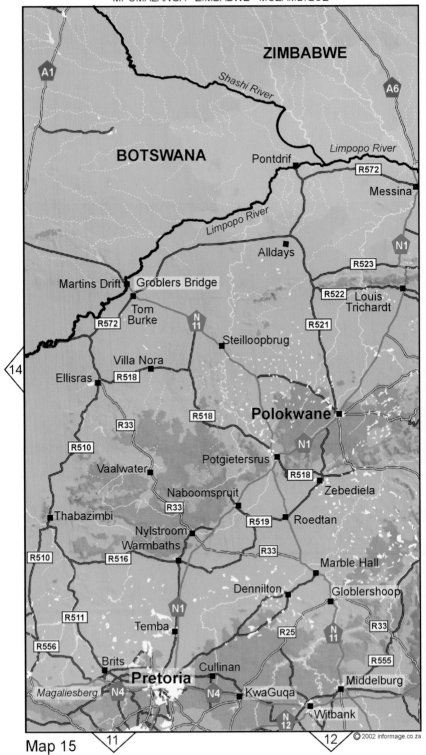

Map 15

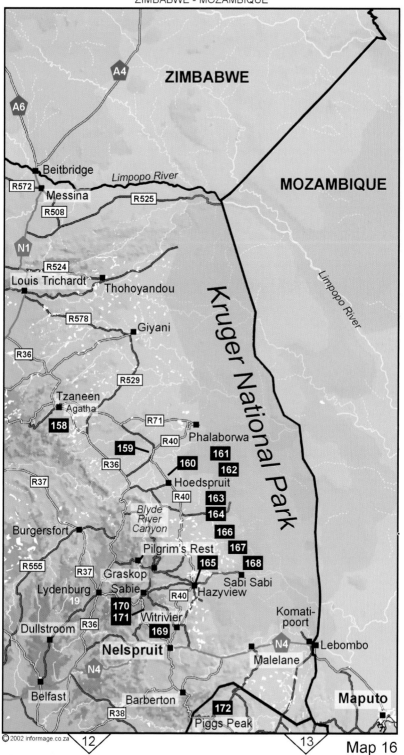

ZIMBABWE

MOZAMBIQUE

Limpopo River

Limpopo River

Kruger National Park

Beitbridge
R572
Messina
R525
R508
N1
R524
Louis Trichardt
Thohoyandou
R578
Giyani
R36
R529
Tzaneen
Agatha
158
R71
R40
Phalaborwa
159
161
160
162
R36
Hoedspruit
R37
R40
163
164
Blyde
River
Canyon
166
Burgersfort
167
Pilgrim's Rest
R555
165
168
R37
Graskop
Lydenburg
Sabie
R40
Sabi Sabi
19
Hazyview
170
171
Komati-
poort
Dullstroom
R36
169
Witrivier
N4
Nelspruit
N4
Lebombo
Malelane
Belfast
N4
Maputo
Barberton
172
R38
Piggs Peak

© 2002 informage.co.za

12

13

Map 16

Western Cape

Froggs Leap

Jôke Glauser
15 Baviaanskloof Rd, Hout Bay, 7806
Tel: 021-790-2590 Fax: 021-790-2590
Email: info@froggsleap.co.za Web: www.froggsleap.co.za
Cell: 082-493-4403

The huge Frogg's Leap verandah, with its impressive views of the Hout Bay mountains and sea seems to be the focal point of life here. At breakfast the house springs to life with Jôke (pronounced yokie) and Stewart engaging in easy banter with all who emerge, and chiding guests for sitting at the long wooden table inside when the parasol-shaded tables outside are so enticing. Then in the evening, with the sea breeze swinging the hammocks and a sundowner in your hand, it is not hard to get to grips with being lazy and on holiday. I can't remember a place where guests made themselves so at home. Jôke and Stewart used to run charter boats in the West Indies and Frogg's Leap has a breezy Caribbean feel with many open french doors and windows. Bedrooms are cool ensembles of natural materials: painted floors, seagrass matting, palms, natural stone in bathrooms, lazy wicker chairs, reed ceilings, thick cotton percale linen and old wooden furniture. Hout Bay itself is a fishing harbour enclosed by mountains and is within minutes of beaches and hiking trails. Jôke and Stewart keep a 26-ft catamaran there and, when the spirit moves them and weather permits, will take guests cray-fishing, or whale-watching when whales are in town. This is a place that has been consistently recommended both before and since the first edition and it is a continued pleasure to recommend it myself.

Rooms: 6: 5 doubles/twins and 1 double, all with en/s bathrooms; 3 with shower, 3 with bath and shower. Plus extra single room.
Price: R200 – R300 pp sharing. Singles on request.
Meals: Full breakfast included and served until 10 am. There are 20 restaurants nearby for other meals.
Directions: A map will be faxed to you on confirmation of booking.

Cape Town, Western Cape

The Houtbay Hideaway

Niels van Reenen
37 Skaife St, Hout Bay, 7806
Tel: 021-790-8040 Fax: 021-790-8114
Email: info@houtbay-hideaway.com
Web: www.houtbay-hideaway.com   Cell: 082-332-7853

Greenwood Guides appraisal forms, while brilliantly designed, do not easily cater for the varied delights of houses such as The Hout Bay Hideaway. By the time I left Niels's magical kingdom I was all but writing on my trousers in an effort to record everything I had seen and heard. Art Deco furniture – lights, *chaise longue*, Bakelite ashtrays, armchairs et al – is the defining motif, but competes for attention with the stunning garden, views, fireplaces, paintings, and Niels, one of Holland's finest. There are three suites and two apartments all abounding in character. Honeymooners will love the double-headed shower of the Garden Apartment, while older-school romantics can fight over the views of the mountains from the aptly-named Skylight Suite. My favourite was the Deco Apartment, with furniture from the Amsterdam school, Zambian sculptures and a discreet outdoor shower where you can munch grapes hanging off the trellis. The house melts into its surroundings because its colour, which attracts strangers in off the street, derives from the garden's eucalyptus tree. Niels does not do things by halves! Want to cool off outside? Choose between pool and fully-plumbed bath. Need a drink? Enjoy the open bar in its 230-year old cupboard. Fancy a drive? Then hire one of the vintage Jaguars. I could go on for hours. *House can be hired in its entirety, children 12+ welcome.*

Rooms: 5: 2 x 2-room apartments (sleeping up to 3); 3 suites sleeping 2. Or this can be converted to a "penthouse" sleeping 6. Or take the entire villa – sleeps 10-12.
Price: R400 – R800 pp sharing. Singles on request. If you take the entire villa it costs from R4800 per day.
Meals: Breakfast included. Other meals by arrangement, but excellent restaurants in Hout Bay!
Directions: Emailed or faxed on booking. Car rental company can pick up from and deliver to the airport or Niels will fetch you in one of the vintage Jags.

Hattons

Liz and Kevin Davis

2 Harold Close, Oakhurst Estate, Hout Bay, 7806
Tel: 021-790-0848 Fax: 021-790-3050
Email: liz@hattons.co.za Web: www.hattons.co.za
Cell: 082-760-2624

From the outside you might not expect too much of this door in a keyhole close. But once inside the building's true dimensions reveal themselves, a great surprise with breezy open spaces and a cavernous sitting room with pole beams and steepling thatched roof. Doors open on both sides, one leading to the pool and the other out to the view over the back of Table Mountain and their own garden. This is immaculately laid out with paths that wind past tropical blooms, a goldfish pond, a vine arbour… and this is also where the rooms, named after trees – strelitzia, mimosa, kumassi – are kept. Not so much rooms as little cottages, with their own doors out to the garden and kitchenettes with sink, washing machine and fridge. The most popular has an unusual gallery bedroom, which looks down on its own sitting room from a height. Kevin and Liz are a young couple, and dedicated to their guests. They (Kevin, Liz, the baby and two friendly dogs) welcome you in with wine, OJ or coffee and they often have a braai for guests who stay more than a couple of nights. Listen carefully when they are spilling the beans about the best spots on the Garden Route!

Rooms: 4: 3 apartments (self-catering or B&B) and 1 B&B double with en suite shower. All have en suite shower & bath.
Price: R250 – R300 pp sharing. Singles R350 – R450. Less R40 if you don't have breakfast.
Meals: Self-catering possible.
Directions: Emailed or faxed on booking.

Villa Jacqui

Merrick and Jacqui Goddard
3 Chilton Close, Hout Bay, 7800
Tel: 021-790-6306 Fax: 021-790-8597
Email: mgoddard@mweb.co.za Web: www.villajacqui.co.za
Cell: 082-456-4333

If you want to splash out on a bit of luxury during your time in Cape Town, then Villa Jacqui provides an excellent setting for some serious pampering. Merrick makes no apologies for the fact that he and Jacqui do not actually need to run a guest house. But having built this superb mustard-coloured mansion on the hillside above Hout Bay in 1999, and having decided that it was actually too big for them, they thought they might as well turn one of their main pleasures – entertaining friends – into a way of life. Consequently, guests become part of the family for the duration of their stay, yet have their every need attended to. The house is situated on land that the Goddards reclaimed from the forest on the slopes of Chimney Mountain and is one of the highest dwellings in Hout Bay. The large pool, the benches dotted around the steeply-banked garden, the verandah at sunset, all provide a wealth of viewpoints from which to admire one of Cape Town's finest vistas. And should you manage to drag yourself inside through the sitting rooms, the bedrooms are palatial. All have extra-length king-sized beds, hand-painted walls and underfloor heating; the level of furnishing throughout redefines the term 'plush'. *Ask about children.*

Rooms: 3: 2 doubles and 1 suite, all with en suite separate showers and baths.
Price: R990 – R1550 pp sharing. No single supplement.
Meals: Full breakfast included. The price also includes a salad lunch and a three-course dinner (whether you want them or not).
Directions: On brochure or faxed. One word of advice: ignore the no entry sign at the top of Andrews Road and drive up to Villa Jacqui that way.

Les Cascades de Bantry Bay

Luc and Els Deschouwer

48 De Wet Road, Bantry Bay, 8005
Tel: 021-434-5209
Fax: 021-439-4206
Email:
fontain@gem.co.za
Web:
www.lescascades.co.za

Les Cascades plummets down the steep side of a hill high up in Bantry Bay, presenting the wide-eyed initiate with a new surprise (or several) at every step. Three slim gentlemen in fezzes (painted wood-carvings from Cairo) greeted me as I made my way downstairs to meet the delightful – and irrepressibly creative – Deschouwers. Kudu-leather sofas and zebra-skin stools sit around an old Thai cart with brass and leather fittings which, minus wheels, has become a low coffee table. An intricately-carved Goan door and frame act as gateway to the drinks cabinet, and the whole room opens out onto a large sundeck and rim-flow pool. There is also a thirteen-metre pool below the house. Next door is the large dining room, though you can also eat meals out on the deck. Each of the other floors has two rooms, which echo the earthy colours and themes in the main living area. Let's not mince words, they are exquisite. All have huge beds and balconies and share the same spectacular view, which I nearly forgot to mention (a measure of Luc and Els' achievements with the house): the sea, the bay, and a heavenly sunset.

Rooms: 6: all doubles with en suite bath and separate shower.
Price: R675 – R850 pp sharing. Single supplement R300.
Meals: Full breakfast included. Meals are available à la carte.
Directions: Faxed or emailed when you book.

Atlantic View

Greg Boki and Rainer Pires
31 Francolin Rd, Camps Bay, 8005
Tel: 021-438-2254 or 0207-724-9800 in UK Fax: 021-438-1273 or
in UK 0207-724-0099 Email: info@atlanticviewcapetown.com
Web: www.atlanticviewcapetown.com Cell: 072-228-1810

Is this how film stars live? I think so. Greg and Rainer have really splashed out and turned this Camps Bay house into a luxury pad. Guests live on the downstairs level of the two-storey house overlooking the pool and sea. Three rooms have the pure sea view – Greg is even busy burying the electricity line at the back so guests don't have to look at anything so mundane – while the fourth room looks up at the mountain behind the house. Bedrooms are slick and chic: travertine floors, modern bright local art, orthopaedically comfortable beds, finest linen, silk cushions scattered with care, safes hidden in cupboards, bathrobes…. It's all swishly state-of-the-art, the *dernier cri* of the interiors magazines that are queuing up to photograph the place. Bathrooms are also modern with frameless glass and side-jets in the showers and a sort of cascade-effect tap in the baths. The rooms all open onto an outside space, where you can have breakfast if you choose or you can have it in the sitting-cum-dining room inside (also stylish and modern with satellite TV, DVDs and CD). When I visited the garden had just been created. Palm trees were flown in by a 60-tonne crane no less (as Greg says "It gave a whole new meaning to Sunday afternoon gardening") and there are koy ponds and tropical plants. There's also an overflow pool, surrounded by smart chaises longues, so get your sunglasses on and dream of Hollywood!

Rooms: 4: all doubles, 1 with en/s bath and shower, 1 with en/s shower, 1 with private b and sh, 1 with private steam shower. All have aircon and underfloor heating.
Price: R325 – R850 pp sharing depending on the room and the season.
Meals: Full breakfast with evening apéritifs and hors d'oeuvres included. Light meals on request. Or you can BBQ. Camps Bay is rich in restaurants.
Directions: Ask when you book or visit the web site.

Ocean View House

Nicole Stephens
33 Victoria Rd, Bakoven, 8005
Tel: 021-438-1982 Fax: 021-438-2287
Email: oceanview@mweb.co.za Web: www.oceanview-house.com

There's no end to Ocean View's eccentric delights – Russian marble, Malawian fish, award-winning gardens. Everyone has either a balcony or a terrace with fabulous views of both the sea and the Twelve Apostle mountains that line up behind the hotel. It is a hotel I suppose, but such a personal one. And there's humour here too: a kitsch-but-fun zebra room, a two-ton statue of an elephant in the water fantasia garden, its trunk reaching up into one of the 200-year-old milkwood trees. Of course there is a great pool, and how many hotels run an honesty bar? To cap it all, Ocean View has its own nature reserve, a tropical garden that ushers an idyllic river from the mountains to the sea. They have placed tables and sun-loungers on the grassy river banks, a sort of exotic Wind in the Willows scenario with rocks, lily pads, ferns, trees, tropical birds and butterflies. If you ever feel like leaving Ocean View, Camps Bay beach is a stroll away with its string of outdoor restaurants and zesty atmosphere. A special place indeed.

Rooms: 13: 1 'presidential', 5 'royal' and 7 'luxury' (all sea-facing).
12 have showers , 1 with bath.
Price: From R450 – R2500 pp sharing. Singles R525 – R5000.
Meals: Full breakfast is included and served until 10.30 am.
Group meals by prior arrangement.
Directions: On the coast road a mile out of Camps Bay towards
Hout Bay.

Brenda's Guest House

Brenda Furman
14 Pine Rd, Green Point, 8005
Tel: 021-434-0902 Fax: 021-434-0109
Email: brendas@mweb.co.za Web: www.brendas.co.za
Cell: 083-627-5583

From the green brick garden terrace this early 1900s house juts forward like the prow of a ship and Brenda has done nothing to dispel the image. Life-saving buoys, fishing nets and oars cling to the surrounding walls. Guests sit out here for *al fresco* evening drinks round the pool from the 'honesty' bar (sherry and port are on the house by the way). Rooms inside are bright and cheerful in wicker, tiles and wood, while quilts, sunflowers and oil paintings add plenty of vivid colour. The rest of the interior space is open-plan: a sitting room with white sofas and glass coffee table, and the dining table where breakfasts are taken all together (breakfast also makes its appearance outside on fine mornings). Brenda makes the breakfast herself (including specials), serving through a marble-topped hatch, so she can spend at least some of the day helping you out with things to do. She patrols the Cape countryside on her huge motorbike gaining first-hand knowledge of where to go and what to do. A very friendly base indeed... Purdy, Brenda's minuscule dog, has not grown much since I last saw her. *Golf, the Waterfront shopping complex and the city centre are all close by.*

Rooms: 5: 1 twin in outside cottage, 2 doubles and 2 twins in the house; all with en suite shower or bath and shower.
Price: R240 – R290 pp sharing. Singles R340 – R490. 5% discount for cash.
Meals: Breakfast included and served until 9 am.
Directions: Ask Brenda to fax her map when booking.

Huijs Haerlem

Johan du Preez and Kees Burgers
25 Main Drive, Sea Point, 8005
Tel: 021-434-6434 Fax: 021-439-2506
Email: haerlem@iafrica.com Web: www.huijshaerlem.co.za

Don't even try and pronounce it! Imagine, it used to be called 't Huijs Haerlem, so small thanks for small mercies! But what a great place: a secret garden, perched high on the hill above Sea Point, enclosed behind walls and gates, abloom with tropical flowers in beds and earthenware pots, with suntrap lawns, a pool (salt-water, solar-heated), and views over Table Bay. The verandah frame is snaked about with vine and small trees provide the shade. Johan and Kees have a lovely, caring approach to their guests and look after you royally. There's no formal reception area, the bar is based on honesty, all their fine Dutch and South African antiques are not hidden away for fear of breakage. In fact both of them suffer from magpie-itis and walls and surfaces teem with eye-arresting objects: a tailor's mannequin, cabinet-making tools, old linen presses. Of course breakfast is enormous with fresh breads, rolls and croissants, fruits, cheeses, cold meats and the full cooked bonanza. This is Johan's domain, a chance for him to banter with guests and make a few suggestions. All the bedrooms are different, but all have their advantage, some with private terraces, some great views, one a four-poster. Whichever room you are in you will feel part of the whole.

Rooms: 8: 5 twins and 3 doubles; all en suite, 2 with separate bath and shower, the rest with shower over bath.
Price: R325 – R500 pp sharing. Singles R400 – R600.
Meals: Full breakfast included.
Directions: Faxed or emailed on booking.

Lézard Bleu Guest House

Chris and Niki Neumann
30 Upper Orange St, Oranjezicht, 8001
Tel: 021-461-4601 Fax: 021-461-4657
Email: welcome@lezardbleu.co.za Web: www.lezardbleu.co.za

It's going to be hard to book the treehouse, particularly when word gets round, but you have got to try! Surely the most wonderful bedroom in Cape Town. The trunks of two giant palm trees spear through a wooden deck at vertiginous heights and a tiny balcony is in among the topmost fronds and spikes. Lezard Bleu was just about the best guest house in Cape Town anyway, so this latest extravagant addition represents one great big cherry on a mouthwatering cake. Niki is an actress and Chris is a chef, although he has hung up his hat now... no, don't even ask! They are still young and humorous and the house remains sleek and modern with solid maplewood bedframes, white pure cotton, sandy shades and tones, bright splashes of local and modern art on the walls. Breakfast is the best beanfeast in Cape Town (and that's the opinion of other guest house owners). The Blue Lizard snakes pleasingly from area to area, each room with its own doors out to a patio and to the large pool, where deck loungers take it easy on a patch of lawn. There are real fires in winter, an honesty bar, chauffeur service – mere details, but typical. Individual, creative, very comfortable, but most importantly this is somewhere really natural and friendly.

Rooms: 7: 1 family room; 5 doubles/twins; 4 with en/s bath and sh; 1 with en/s sh; 1 treehouse double en/s b and sh.
Price: R350 – R600 pp sharing. Singles +50%.
Meals: Full breakfast included and served till 10.30 am.
Directions: Ask for directions when booking.

Montague House

Janet and Stephen Edds

18 Leeuwenhof Road,
Higgovale, 8001
Tel: 021-424-7337
Fax: 021-426-0423
Email:
info@montaguehouse.net
Web:
www.montaguehouse.net

An enclave in the lee of Table Mountain, Montague House is secluded behind walls in recherché Higgovale, a modern take on a Tuscan villa with rough, washed walls, terracotta paving and a pool offered shade by the frangipani tree. The interior main room is a large open-plan sitting room, office, kitchen and breakfast room with great solid beams, tiled floor and the Italian theme is taken up in old master blow-up prints on walls (Botticelli's Birth of Venus for example). There are just five rooms all lightly themed according to a Shakespeare play (don't worry, they haven't plumped for Titus Andronicus or Macbeth!), and centred round grand four-poster beds draped with mosquito netting that is both ornate and functional. No corners have been cut in designing and fitting out bathrooms with glass cubicle showers and separate bath, and some lovely volcanic limestone tiles. Upstairs rooms have balconies with views of the mountain and all the rooms are blessed with space-age, flat-screen TVs, intriguing to the uninitiated. Stephen and Janet are a British couple, sharing the house with their guests, offering a great deal of good advice on your onward trip, and expert on wines. They stock a Top Twenty wine list that keeps abreast of reality rather than notoriety! Wine buffs are extremely welcome. Stephen is also an accomplished chef and dinners are eaten en famille. During the life of the guide two more rooms are being built.

Rooms: 5: all king-size four-posters, 4 with en suite bath and shower, 1 with en suite shower.
Price: R600 – R900 pp sharing. Singles on request.
Meals: Full breakfast included. Dinners by request: about R120 a head (order by 10 same morning).
Directions: Emailed or faxed on booking.

Liberty Lodge

Jimmy van Tonder
33 De Lorentz St, Tamboerskloof, 8001
Tel: 021-423-2264 Fax: 021-423-2274
Email: liberty@capetowncity.co.za Web: www.capetowncity.co.za

Liberty Lodge is an African colonial townhouse alright, built in 1894 as a bachelor pad… but it is original in more ways than one. The sense of colour and humour are equally deft and any gravitas associated with the Victorian era is gently undermined. Hunting prints, for example, are sent up by empty wire heads of impala and kudu mounted on bedroom walls. There are appealing objects from all over the world to brighten the day… Indian and Thai artefacts, West African hairdresser's shop signs in brightest oils and silver frames, and there are some fun colour schemes, mauve and green stripes for example. Bathrooms are sometimes small, but inventive use of space sees one upstairs room with a glass-bead curtain and an Indian carved cupboard embedded in the wall. There are wooden floors with painted motifs throughout the house, and two of the upstairs rooms walk out onto a verandah with tables, chairs and views of Table Mountain. Classical music plays unobtrusively in the background throughout the day and Jimmy is there to recommend a restaurant over a glass of wine in the evening. Breakfast finally is either out in the courtyard or at the highly polished dining table. Buckets of character and comfort at Liberty Lodge. *TV (MNET) and personal telephones in bedrooms. Airport transfer can be arranged.*

Rooms: 4: all doubles/twins, 3 with en suite shower, 1 with en suite bath.
Price: R225 – R325 pp sharing. Singles R350 – R450.
Meals: Full breakfast included.
Directions: Faxed or emailed on booking.

Acorn House

Bernd Schlieper and Beate Lietz

1 Montrose Avenue, Oranjezicht, 8001
Tel: 021-461-1782 Fax: 021-461-1768
Email: welcome@acornhouse.co.za Web: www.acornhouse.co.za

Bernd and Beate can barely contain the happiness they derive from Acorn House, and their enthusiasm rubs off quickly on all but the stoniest of their visitors. I was a pushover. The listed building, designed by busy Sir Herbert Baker in 1904, sits on the sunny, sea-facing slopes of Table Mountain with tip-top views to Table Bay. The house is typical Sir Herbert, timber colonnade, broad verandah et al, and there is an immaculate garden with black-slate swimming pool, and a sun-lounging lawn, cleanly demarcated by agapanthus and lavender bushes. Breakfast, often served by the pool, is a no-holds-barred display of meats, cheeses, eggs and freshly-squeezed fruit juices; "probably the second-best breakfast in Cape Town" is Beate's carefully-worded claim! Upstairs, in your wood-floored bedroom you will find welcome notes, or farewell notes, chocolates and sprigs of lavender. Wine-lovers are also well served: Bernd is *pazzo* for the stuff, and regularly visits local vineyards to ensure that his house wines are up-to-the-moment (just for his guests' benefit, of course). Bernd and Beate have only been living in South Africa since October 2000 and are awash with excitement about their new surroundings. A stay in Acorn House will leave you feeling much the same.

Rooms: 8: 1 king; 3 twins and 3 doubles all with en suite bath; 1 family suite with twin.
Price: R340 – R490 pp sharing. Singles R440 – R590.
Meals: Full breakfast included.
Directions: See web site or ask for fax.

Map Number 1

Redbourne Hilldrop

Jonny and Sharon Levin
12 Roseberry Avenue, Oranjezicht, 8001
Tel: 021-461-1394 Fax: 021-465-1006
Email: info@redbourne.co.za Web: www.redbourne.co.za

One of the happiest and most humorous guest houses in Cape Town, so it always seems to me. Many of Jonny and Sharon's guests refuse to stay elsewhere and gifts arrive daily from overseas... well almost. One day you may be surprised to find yourself packing up toys for their kids. It's a small, intimate place and you are spoiled: free-standing baths, fluffy duvets, big white pillows, unflowery good taste in mirrors and wood floors, magazines, African artefacts, great showers. One room has a spiral staircase down to its bathroom. You eat breakfast at a diner-style bar, stretched along a wall of pretty windows with incredible city views. Guests are treated as far as possible as friends and each time I visit I notice the easy rapport that Jonny and Sharon have generated with their guests – probably overnight. Last edition I said that a wall-enclosed pool would be ready for this edition, but I didn't really believe it. "It wouldn't matter if it wasn't". I said hedging my bets. Well, lo and behold, there it is, with Table Mountain looming above as suggested it might!

Rooms: 4: 2 doubles and 1 twin; 2 with en/s bath and shower, 1 with en/s sh. And 1 family room with sunroom (pictured above).
Price: R275 – R375 pp sharing. Singles R375 – R475.
Meals: Full breakfast included. Dinners by prior arrangement.
Directions: Ask when booking.

Trevoyan Guest House

Dee Millner

12 Gilmour Hill Rd, Tamboerskloof, 8001
Tel: 021-424-4407 Fax: 021-423-0556
Email: trevoyan@iafrica.com Web: www.trevoyan.co.za

Guests are free-range at this relaxed colonial-style guest house. You can wander into the kitchen, stroll on the wide verandah or have breakfast there, too, in full view of the mountain. There's something cool and self-contained about Trevoyan that cossets you from the noise and heat of the surrounding city. I particularly liked the happy-coloured morning room with its Oregon pine floor and the bright garden suites with their own sitting rooms. All the guest bedrooms are large with thick carpets (underfloor heating in winter), duvets and fluffed up pillows, TVs hidden in wooden cabinets and a basket of soaps and shampoos for the bathroom. There is a pool, of course, log fires in winter, flowers, African music... and the whole edifice is watched over by a venerable and highly cherished old oak tree. Finally parents are well catered for at Trevoyan, quite rare for Cape Town. There are convertible sofa beds (in the garden suites) for kids and even babysitting laid on, so you can actually go out in the evening. Imagine…!

Rooms: 6: 4 doubles/twins in main house; 2 garden suites (1 twin and 1 double); all with en suite bath and shower.
Price: R315 – R420 pp sharing. Singles R430 – R600. Suites R600 – R900 per room flat rate.
Meals: Full breakfast included and served when you want it (within reason). No evening meals cooked here but can organize meals to be brought in.
Directions: Ask for directions when booking.

Medindi Manor

Geoffrey Bowman, Leshira and Basetsana Mosaka
4 Thicket Road, Rosebank, 7700
Tel: 021-686-3563 Fax: 021-686-3563
Email: manor@medindi.co.za Web: www.medindi.co.za
Cell: 082-658-9955

Medindi is a secluded Edwardian manor of grand dimensions, banded by ground and first-floor verandahs with a garden and swimming pool tucked away behind tall hedges and bushes. Some of the rooms have their own doors out onto the stoep and the main building has been renovated with panache and a sensitive feel for the period. Although well-stocked with bar fridges, telephones, TVs etc, Medindi avoids like the plague any h(ot)ellish homogeneity in its décor and design. The Oregon pine floors, bay windows, intricate ceilings and marble fireplaces are original and there are unique, antique touches everywhere, such as Edwardian designs for stately marble and slate floors. Bathrooms have free-standing baths, Victorian 'plate' shower heads, brass fittings and a small antique cabinet has been found for each. There is modernity too, in bright wall colours (yellows and blues), and splashes of modern art – from the turn of one century to the turn of the next. Music is an important ingredient for Geoffrey, Medindi's owner. He plays the piano (there was and will be again a grand in the huge breakfast room) and the house attracts many musicians as guests. A freewheeling, relaxed and youthful place. Since the last edition Leshira and Basetsana have taken over the day-to-day management of Medindi and six new rooms have been created from a converted outbuilding – the smaller rooms are cheaper.

Rooms: 12: in the house: 4 doubles and 2 twins; all with en/s bathrooms, 3 with baths and showers, 3 with showers. Plus 6 more rooms in the converted outbuilding.
Price: R245 – R445 pp sharing. Singles R295 – R595.
Meals: Buffet breakfast included, cooked breakfast extra: R27.50.
Directions: Ask when you book.

Map Number

Vine Bungalow

Eulalie Spamer
7 Ellerslie Rd, Wynberg, 7800
Tel: 021-761-9554 Fax: 021-797-8183
Email: cdspamer@iafrica.com

The Vine Bungalow (and that's 'bungalow' in the colonial, wrought-iron-verandah sort of sense) is an opportunity (if you can get in) to live far more stylishly than I can see myself managing ever! Everywhere you look the finest of the fine gazes evenly back: shiny wood floors, Jim Thompson fabrics, embroidered white cotton sheets, a glass-box shower in a marble bathroom, a 'five-star mandi' as Eulalie describes a marble-encased square pool-bath. And all the kitchen and washing appliances are aristocrats and top of their range. All these basics are a pleasure in themselves. But Eulalie has created a home, and guests are treated to the full force of her great taste for interiors and a wonderful collection of art and artefacts to boot. You take the whole house and self-cater so it will suit longer-stayers or families best. Guests are provided with a light meal on arrival (fruits, cheeses, rôtisserie chicken and a bottle of wine for example) but thereafter you will need to get down to a supermarket – it's 500 metres to Wynberg Village. Eulalie lives next door so is on hand to help you settle in. A family had just arrived from the UK and were out on the breakfasting stoep by the swimming pool when I visited. They looked …delighted.

Rooms: 1 house with 3 bedrooms, 2 with en suite bathrooms (1 shower and 1 'five-star mandi').
Price: R1200 – R1800 a day for the house.
Meals: Light meal on arrival. Otherwise self-catering.
Directions: Off M3 Trovato Link pass Herschel Walk turn-off. After Herschel Walk it's the 4th road to your left.

Klein Bosheuwel

Nicki Scarborough
51a Klaassens Rd, Constantia, 7806
Tel: 021-762-2323 Fax: 021-762-2323
Email: kleinbosheuwel@iafrica.com
Web: www.kleinbosheuwel.co.za

Who needs Kirstenbosch? Nicki has manipulated the paths and lawns of her own garden (which is pretty well an extension of the Botanical Gardens anyway – less than a minute's walk away) so that the views are not dished out in one vulgar dollop! Instead you are subtly led into them, with glimpses through mature trees (flowering gums, yellowwoods and camellias) and lush flower beds. And finally your stroll leads you down to umbrellas on a ridge with Table Mountain and the Constantiaberg laid out magnificently before you and the sea distantly below. "Keep it plain" is Nicki's motto, so the upstairs bedrooms are simply white, and all naturally endowed with garden views. The salt-water swimming pool is hidden deep in the garden and Klein Bosheuwel is the sort of place where you could just hang out for a few days. I was introduced to one English guest who had clearly no intention of going anywhere that day – the cat that got the cream you might have thought! *Ask when booking about children.*

Rooms: 4: 1 twin en/s bath; 2 doubles with en/s bath and shower; 1 double en/s large bath.
Price: R265 – R340 pp sharing. Singles R400 – R500.
Meals: Full breakfast included. Can organise other meals on request.
Directions: Fax or web site.

Almond Hill House

Lesley Arnot
9 Avenue Beauvais, Klaassenbosch Drive, Constantia, 7806
Tel: 021-794-6150 Fax: 021-794-0975
Email: lesarnot@iafrica.com
Cell: 082-412-6220

Just one room, but what a place! Start with the bathroom…you won't find many better in South Africa, enough space for a large bedroom. Naturallly there are both shower (glass-fronted) and bath (vaulted and candlelit), a stone floor and the demurer tones are offset by a single bright Gauguinesque painting. And the bedroom itself has been mulled over in detail for your greatest possible happiness: percale linen, huge bed, antique furniture, armchairs and table, satellite TV, fridge. And two stable-style doors, one leading towards the fabulous (still maturing) gardens, the other onto a stoep, the stage upon which breakfast typically is enacted (but it's your choice). You will enjoy the view. The house was only recently built on high ground and in the distance the walls of mountains sweep round until the Hottentots Holland drop into the sea at Gordon's Bay… and of course there's False Bay itself. While in the foreground a rectangular swimming pool sits in a wide expanse of lawn (6000 square metres). Guests are welcome to use the pool too and you can walk off onto trails from the house. Lesley's métier is interior design, but her exterior designs (i.e. the gardens and the house) ain't bad either. You will be well looked after, don't you worry.

Rooms: 1 double with en suite bath and shower. Underfloor heating.
Price: R225 – R325 pp sharing. Singles R350 – R550
Meals: Full breakfast included. Braais on request R95 a head.
Directions: Ask when booking.

Dendron

Shaun and Jill McMahon

21 Ou Wingerd Pad, Upper Constantia, 7806
Tel: 021-794-6010 Fax: 021-794-2532
Email: dendron@intekom.co.za
Cell: 082-4911-647

Dendron (Gk = tree) lives up to its name: oaks and pines fill the wonderful view down to Groot Constantia through the vineyards and up into the mountain to the right (ask Jill about walks into the vineyards from the garden). There are two cosy cottages in the lawny, leafy, jasmine-scented garden with sitting rooms, kitchenettes, two bedrooms apiece and its own small secluded garden area – perfect for families. A third room sits off the main house. The decoration is simple and appealing: terracotta tiles or wooden floors and beds covered in Indian flower prints. On cold days there are working fireplaces or stoves, and a large brick-surround swimming pool for warmer weather. Each cottage is fully serviced with laundry, phone/fax, TV (with M-Net), private garden and braai. Garden, pool and view together make an enticing picture and induce vacant or pensive mood. Guests often walk off from the gate in the garden to the vineyard-bound Jonkershuys restaurant for dinner, and back again by moon- and torchlight. *Constantia has many excellent restaurants. Satellite TV.*

Rooms: 5 in total: 2 cottages with 1 double and 1 twin each, both with bath and shower; 1 twin with shower.
Price: R140 – R275 pp sharing. Singles on request.
Meals: Full breakfast extra R20 – R30 served until 10 am.
Directions: Fax on request.

Kaapse Draai

Annelie Posthumus

19 Glen Avenue, Constantia, 7806
Tel: 021-794-6291 Fax: 021-794-6291
Email: kaapsedraai@hotmail.com
Cell: 082-923-9869

To really encounter a city like Cape Town you should experience both its urban and wild sides. And at Kaapse Draai you are on the edge of both in the suburbs of Constantia. You can walk from the tropical-style garden with its mountain stream, huge ferns and palms into Bel-Ombre meadow and the forest. From there it is a three-hour walk to the Table Mountain cable station. Porcupines come into the garden at night from the mountain (they love arum lilies apparently) and there are many birds too, including the noisy (and palindromic) hadedah. Or you can drive down to the Constantia Village shopping centre where your more urban urges can be satisfied. One bedroom is up a little staircase with a window seat and small balcony overlooking the garden, but all three are bright with paintings and kilims. Eat summer breakfasts outside to classical music and enjoy Annelie's infectious sense of humour. *Closed 7th Dec to 8th Jan roughly.*

Rooms: 3: 1 double and 2 twins with en suite shower.
Price: R225 – R260 pp sharing. Singles R275 – R310.
Meals: Full breakfast included. Annelie sometimes cooks if the mood is upon her. But do not expect this....
Directions: Ask for fax when booking.

Lusthof

Judy Badenhorst

Roseway, Constantia, 7848
Tel: 021-794-6598 or at the Café 021-794-3010 Fax: 021-794-6598 or -2920 Email: rivercafe@netactive.co.za
Cell: 083-412-3455

Everyone in the world seems to know Judy, whether through the Old Cape Farm Stall, from Buitenverwachting wine estate… or in our case through obscure family links in Britain. You probably know her yourself. All her projects seem to be touched by magic and become social temples for the Constantia faithful. We spent our first two weeks in South Africa staying in her guest cottage in the garden and it was a terrible moment when we finally had to leave the nest and look after ourselves. The cottage, with TV, heaters for winter and kitchenette, has doors onto its own patio, where you can lie on sunloungers and admire the flower garden. Judy is truly a maestro in the kitchen and runs the Spaanschemat River Café at Constantia Uitsig during the day (where you will have breakfast); but she will do all she can to help her guests orientate themselves before and after work. You shouldn't choose Lusthof if you are after a fully-catered guest house with 24-hour service. But if you like to feel part of the furniture, and among friends, then this is the place for you. Mention must finally be made of Chebe, Judy's huge, shaggy, good-natured, lemon-loving bouvier – an integral part of the set-up. Chebe is a dog by the way. *Airport pick-up and car rental can be organised. There has been some talk of installing a plunge pool; better ask Judy.*

Rooms: 1 twin with private bathroom with shower and a kitchenette.
Price: R250 – R350 pp sharing.
Meals: Full breakfast included. You either drive down to the Spaanschemat River Café or materials are provided for you to cook for yourself.
Directions: Ask when booking for a full map.

Vygeboom Manor

Callie & Luli Hamman

14 Valmar Rd, Valmary Park, Durbanville, 7550
Tel: 021-975-6020 Fax: 021-976-5029
Email: vygeboom@gtrade.co.za Web: www.vygeboom.co.za
Cell: 083-270-4021

Vygeboom is a destination in itself. Callie is a prosthodontist and microlight pilot, Luli an artist and these disparate talents merge seamlessly to create a fantastic guest house experience in Cape Town's northern suburbs. Durbanville is an ideal location for visitors, with easy access to the bright lights and beaches of Cape Town, but also on established wine routes (including the ruling triumvirate of Paarl, Stellenbosch and Franschhoek). Prisoners of the game of golf will also find themselves embarrassed for choice. But this assumes, of course, that you feel like going anywhere. Luli has based the themes of each amazing room on her own gigantic and wonderful murals, doffing the cap to Rubens, Matisse, Manet etc. Comfort, however, does not play second fiddle to artistic whimsy – beds are huge, bathrooms luxurious. Add to this charming hosts (Callie does his dentistry next door), spectacular views to the distant wall of the Hottentots Holland Mountains, a vast sitting room with a three-quarter size snooker table, a large pool in the garden and a resident owl who sings in the bluegum at night. *Callie is a microlight pilot and organizes trips for guests – an exciting way to go whale-spotting in season.*

Rooms: 5: 1 double, 4 twins, 3 with en suite bath, 2 with en/s shower.
Price: R300 – R400 pp sharing. Single supplement R400 – R550.
Meals: Full breakfast included and dinners by arrangement.
Directions: Junction 23 N1, R302 north for 5 km. Turn right into Valmar Rd.

Kersefontein

Julian Melck
between Hopefield and Velddrif, Hopefield, 7355
Tel: 022-783-0850 Fax: 022-783-0850
Email: info@kersefontein.co.za Web: www.kersefontein.co.za
Cell: 083-454-1025

Nothing has changed at Kersefontein since the last edition. Julian's convivial dinner parties are still a reason to book in on their own. And Julian himself remains a Renaissance man, described on his business card as 'Farmer, Pig-killer, Aviator and Advocate of the High Court of S.A.' He farms cows, sheep and horses on the surrounding fields, and wild boar appear deliciously at dinner. He also hires and pilots a six-seater plane and a flight round the Cape or along the coast is a must. He modestly leaves out his virtuosity as a pianist and organist and some of us trooped off one Sunday morning, braving a forty-minute sermon in Afrikaans, to hear toccatas by Bach, Giguot and Widor at the local church. When not eating, riding or flying, guests lounge on the pontoon, swim in the river, or read books from Kersefontein's many libraries. Or they use the house as a base to visit the coast, or the Swartland wineries, which are really taking off. The homestead is seventh generation and the rooms either Victorian or African in temperament, with antiques handed down by previous Melcks. You are fed like a king, but treated as a friend and I am always recommending people to go there.

Rooms: 6: 3 doubles and 3 twins; 1 with shower, 2 with bath and 3 with bath and shower.
Price: R330 – R430 pp sharing. No supplement for singles. Aircraft hire prices vary depending on the trip.
Meals: Full breakfast is included. Dinners by arrangement: R120 – R150 excluding wine.
Directions: From CT take N7 off N1. Bypass Malmesbury, 5 km later turn left towards Hopefield. After 50 km bypass Hopefield, turn R signed Velddrif. 16 km house signed on R just before grain silos.

Map Number 2

Klipvlei

Evert and Nadia Basson

Moorreesburg, 7310
Tel: 022-433-2401 Fax: 022-433-2401
Email: klipvlei@wcaccess.co.za

The old farmhouses at Klipvlei form a tightly-knit courtyard, stoeps running like cloisters around a rectangular swimming pool. The buildings are buffered by an expanse of green lawn from the harsher, dryer farmland that surrounds this oasis. This garden teems with birds, including Nadia's white turkeys and geese, and you can pass a contemplative hour or two on resting seats in places of dark shade under cypress trees. The guest house is deep and cool too, with low doorways, thick whitewashed walls, long vine-shaded stoeps, Oregon pine ceilings, alcove fireplaces with wooden lintels and marble-tiled bathrooms. But the antique is wonderfully contrasted by Nadia's boldly-painted walls and modern paintings, while Evert taught himself how and then made all the ironwork pieces in the house (candleholders and lamps etc). Nadia's son is a bird enthusiast and keeps two aviaries of bijou love-birds, budgerigars, doves, parrots and… actually those are the only ones I know the names of! Dinners are often braais on the verandah, eaten *en famille*, and kids (by age or inclination) will love the pool, games room and garden. Evert will take you out on the 500 hectares of wheat, sheep and cattle farm in his bakkie if you ask. This is a very friendly place that you will want to make your home. Base yourself here and visit the sea, mountains and vineyards on day-trips. *Closed Christmas to New Year.*

Rooms: 5: 2 twins, 2 doubles, 1 family room; 2 with en/s shower and bath, 1 en/s shower, 2 share a bathroom with bath and shower.
Price: R150 – R200 pp sharing. R180 – R250 for singles.
Meals: Full breakfast included. Lunch and dinners available in an excellent restaurant nearby. Or Nadia will cook for no fewer than 4 in the evening.
Directions: From Cape Town take N1 then N7 North for about 100 km – it is signed left to Moorreesburg. Go straight through town and you will see signs to the farm on the right.

Langebaan Beach House

Claire Green
44 Beach Road, Entrance in Jacoba St, Langebaan, 7357
Tel: 022-772-2625 Fax: 022-772-1432
Email: lbh@intekom.co.za Web: www.langebaaninfo.com/beach

The Langebaan Beach House was once Claire's family's seaside retreat in the days when Langebaan was a small fishing village. It has grown since then, but still has a nice holiday feel. Claire's place is right on the lagoon with a garden that goes directly down to sand and water. The original part is over 100 years old, the rest has gradually been added as the family expanded – most of it now for guests. Two of the bedrooms are 'suites', with their own sitting rooms (complete with kettle and small fridge) and views to the water. The other two rooms are on the other side of the house by the plunge pool. There is plenty of living space, a big communal sitting room where Claire's collection of model boats lives and the garden has sun-loungers, an iron table and chairs for post-beach relaxing. Decoration throughout is simple and attractive, in keeping with the seaside feel; white-washed walls, terracotta tiles, bright bed covers. Breakfast is served in the glass-enclosed verandah, looking down to the beach. This is a relaxed, seasidey sort of place, with an abundance of restaurants just around the corner. The sea is safe and swimmable by the way – if a little chilly.

Rooms: 4: 2 suites, each with sitting room; 1 double and 1 twin. All rooms have en/s bathrooms with shower.
Price: Suites: R250 – R275 pp sharing. Singles R260. Other rooms: R175 – R200. Singles R200.
Meals: Full breakfast included. For other meals there are lots of great restaurants in Langebaan – 5 within walking distance.
Directions: Directions will be faxed or emailed when you book.

Map Number 2

Blue Dolphin

George Koning
12 Warrelklip St, Paternoster, 7381
Tel: 022-752-2001 Fax: 022-715-1027
Email: bluedolphin@mweb.co.za Web: www.bluedolphin.co.za

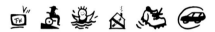

The Blue Dolphin concept is simple, natural and refreshing. Four very comfortable rooms, with views of the sea, a verandah with a day-bed for lying on and listening to the surf, a sandy beach that stretches from the house…and two great restaurants up the road for lunch and dinner. The house is open, wooden, breezy with whites and blues dominating in tune with the beach and sea. All you have to do is lazily watch out for dolphins (and whales in season), kick sand along the strand, eat your breakfast, chat with George, read a book… chill those nerves, untie those muscles. Book early for the flower season (end of August/beginning of September). The dune fynbos blooms impressively and a rash of tiny brightly-coloured flowers emerge like magic from the very sand itself. George has kept the number of rooms down to just four so that he always has plenty of time for everyone. The bedrooms are well kitted-out with heated towel rails, satellite TV, mohair blankets, great beds and linen. Finally this is seafood heaven. Paternoster is extremely lucky to have the Voorstrand restaurant (at the time of writing), meals eaten right down by the sea, a short walk from The Blue Dolphin along the beach. *Columbine Nature Reserve and the Fossil Museum are nearby.*

Rooms: 4: all doubles with en suite shower.
Price: R175 – R200 pp sharing. Singles R300 – R350.
Meals: Full breakfast included. Excellent meals at Voorstrand and Vissermans Kombuis restaurants in Paternoster.
Directions: Directions faxed on booking.

Villa Dauphine

David and Ann Dixon
166 Sandpiper Close, Golden Mile Bvd, Britannia Bay, 7382
Tel: 022-742-1926 Fax: 022-742-1926
Email: dadixon@mweb.co.za Web: www.villadauphine.com
Cell: 083-409-3195

Cosseted within its own walls Villa Dauphine shuns the harsh sandveld of the interior and focuses instead on the bay whose broad arc passes not twenty yards from the stoep. Here you sit and peacefully beat out the rhythm of the waves. Two finned backs breached some thirty metres from shore, my first ever sighting of wild dolphins. David and Anne were unimpressed. The day before great schools of them had been leaping, frolicking, doing crosswords and playing chess right in front of the house. You can take boat rides out to cement the friendship and navigate the Berg River for bird-watching. The house is country cottage pretty, thatched and beamed with solid furniture, pots of fresh flowers, terracotta tiles, lots of whites and woods. Two atticky bedrooms are found up sweet wooden steps, which lead from a flowery, sun-trapping, wind-breaking courtyard. The other is in the house itself. David and Ann are tremendous enthusiasts for the area, pointing guests off to the fossil park, to golf courses, to the West Coast Nature Reserve, to excellent restaurants in the area (fish or steak). And then there is the miracle of the spring flowers. They grow right down to the water line and as Anne says, "where do they come from?"

Rooms: 2 'units': 1 suite with 2 double bedrooms with a shared bathroom (bath & shower). 1 twin with en/s bath and shower.
Price: R165 – R230 pp sharing. Singles R180 – R250.
Meals: Dinner by arrangement: R60.
Directions: From Cape Town R27 to Vredenburg turn-off. Turn L to Vredenburg. First lights, turn R to St. Helena Bay. 12 km to Stompneusbaai sign. Turn L. 17 km turn L to Britannia Bay. 2 km. Turn R at White Entrance to Golden Mile. Turn R and after 2nd speed bump turn L.

Pampoen Fontein

Gemma and Richard Carlsson
Porterville
Tel: 021-689-7792 Fax: 021-689-7792
Email: gemmac@mweb.co.za
Cell: 082-564-5500

I have to admit, just the directions had me salivating on this one. Sure enough, after nine slow kilometres up a winding mountain pass, I found myself torn between two delicious views. To the west I could see across the valley floor to the Piketberg beyond (surely one of the best sunset spots in South Africa), while to the east the late afternoon sun was busy doing wonderful things to the craggy Witsenberg. In its own mini-valley between the two, you'll be very pleased to hear, are Pampoen Fontein's two secluded cottages. Lilly Cottage is an airy, all-wood chalet sleeping four, surrounded by decking and overlooking a small dam – very 'Rocky Mountains'. Protea Cottage is a whitewashed stone building, which sits snugly beneath a small koppie. The views are down the valley to the north-east and out towards the mountains beyond, which glowed red at sunset. The hammock under a vine on the stoep is very inviting, especially after a walk down to the dam a kilometre away (or further afield – the choices are endless). The cottage is simply but stylishly furnished, with flashes of colour and a big fireplace for those winter days. A great wilderness retreat just an hour or so from Cape Town.

Rooms: 2 self-catering cottages: 'Lilly' has 2 bedrooms and 'Protea' also has 2 bedrooms (with sofa beds for extras).
Price: R100 – R200 pp sharing.
Meals: Self-catering.
Directions: Take N7 from CT to Picketburg. 200 yds after the Picketburg turning, turn R onto R44 to Porterville. 15km to T-junction. Turn L. After 3km turn R at sign to Cardow/Dasklip. Dirt road 9.6km. Turn R at Groot Winterhoek Nature Reserve sign. Take it easy up Dasklip Pass (7km). Ignore Beaverlac, continue 4km and turn L at 'Manager's House'. Manager will direct you to cottage.

Dassieklip Cottages

Hedley Peter and Johann Human
Petersfield Guest Farm, Citrusdal, 7340
Tel: 022-921-3316
Email: petersfield@kingsley.co.za Web: www.citrusdal.info/petersfield
Cell: 083-626-5145

After a long, hot day in the car, and not to spare anyone any blushes, it was a great relief to be met by instantly likeable and funny hosts, such are Hedley and Johann. It is Hedley's family farm, citrus and rooibos, the property ranging over the back of the mountain behind the house, with views across the Oliphants River to the Cederberg mountains on the other side of the valley. The two cottages are self-catering and very private. Dassieklip, the longest-standing, is reached down an avenue of oaks, a sweet, wooden mountain cabin secreted in its own kloof. There's a plunge pool to cool off in, and other mod cons such as fridge, TV and CD player. De Kom, on the other hand, has no electricity, and will excite your inner romantic. We're talking hurricane lamps and flares for light and gas for the stove, fridge and hot water. And what a setting, guarded to the front by citrus trees, to the rear by craggy sandstone and looking deep and far from the stoep down the mountain. There is a pool by the cottage filled by natural water running down rocks, a nearby dam (300 metres) to swim in, picnic by or row a boat on. Bring your own food for both cottages although breakfast materials for you to cook can be provided. *Pets welcome.*

Rooms: 2 cottages with 2 bedrooms each.
Price: From R200 (weekdays) to R320 (weekends) per person per night.
Meals: Self-catering but breakfast materials provided in the fridge by prior arrangement.
Directions: From Cape Town 4 km after Citrusdal on your left on the N7 travelling towards Clanwilliam.

Rockwood Cottage

Pam and Noel Mills

Rockwood Farm, PO Box 131, Citrusdal, 7340
Tel: 022-921-3517 Fax: 022-921-3517
Email: amills@new.co.za Web: www.citrusdal.info/rockwood
Cell: 072-222-3344

Rockwood is an extremely beautiful protea farm in the Cederberg highlands, 800 metres above sea level. Both the main house where Pam and Noel live and their large and lovely guest cottage (self-catering) have front stoeps that overlook a succession of dams, the hinterland channelled away for miles and miles by rugged sandstone mountains. The highest peaks of the Sneeuberg Conservancy are often covered with snow in winter. The guest cottage is cradled among giant rocks with the eponymous rockwood trees growing from beneath. And to the front a story-book stream burbles past the stoep and oak tree there. A wide expanse of lawn leads to more treasure. Noel has created a natural rock swimming pool that is filled all year round by a fresh drinkable river that cascades gently over the rocks. A sundowner either in the pool or in the jacuzzi just above allows you time to digest the magnificent view and feel properly smug. Behind this there is a deep gorge and waterfall, an idyllic world of water and rock, full of wild flowers in season with two bush trails cut through natural gardens. Pam and Noel will happily show their guests all there is to do on the property and in the region, still so unspoiled by tourism.

Rooms: 1 cottage with 2 bedrooms, 1 double and 1 twin sharing 1 bath with shower above.
Price: R400 for 2 people. R50 for each extra person. Accommodation for 6 in total.
Meals: Self-catering, but breakfast materials provided on request.
Directions: From N7 into Citrusdal. At fourway intersection in centre of village straight over and up mountain for 7 km. 2nd white gates on your left.

Boschkloof Cottage

Mariet and Doempie Smit
Boschkloof, Citrusdal, 7340
Tel: 022-921-3533 Fax: 022-921-3533
Email: boschkloof@kingsley.co.za Web: www.citrusdal.info/boschkloof
Cell: 082-734-9467

We bumped along six or so sandy kilometres, past orchards of citrus trees and stumbled upon some sort of prelapsarian idyll! A private valley, cocooned in the Sneeuberg Conservancy, in the foothills of the Cederberg, flanked by sandstone mountains, its orange groves watered by a natural stream, the rocks and plants etched in hyper-real clarity by a setting sun. There are Bushman rock art sites, natural pools in the river to cool off in and hiking on mountain trails to be done from the house in the early morning and evening. We parked under an oak tree and were met by Mariet, her two small daughters and two large dogs. On return from a dip in the river we met Doempie and a glass of wine and were soon being treated to crayfish kebabs from the braai, seated under the oak with views up the kloof and a sensational tone to the air. It just made us well to be there, but they say it was entirely the worst time of year (February)! The Smits live in one of the old farmhouses, their guests next door in the other. Although it is a self-catering arrangement, you are in such close proximity that you might as well be at a B&B, except with far more space and privacy. And the cottage? No time for detail – just trust me, it's lovely!

Rooms: I cottage with 2 bedrooms; I double (with extra single) with bathroom with bath and shower and I twin with a small bathroom with a shower. Can sleep 6.
Price: R400 for 2 people. Extra people R80 each.
Meals: Fully equipped kitchen – this is a self-catering cottage. Mariet can provide breakfast materials for you by prior arrangement.
Directions: N7 to Citrusdal – turn into village, go left into Voortrekker Rd and right into Muller St. Carry straight on, it becomes a dirt road, follow it for 7 km.

Mount Ceder

André and Jaen Marais
Grootrivier Farm,
Cederberg, Koue
Bokkeveld, 6836
Tel: 023-317-0113
Fax: 023-317-0543
Email:
mountceder@lando.co.za
Web:
www.mountceder.co.za

Cederberg, Western Cape

Do not lose confidence as you rumble along the dirt roads that lead through the Koue Bokkeveld nature conservancy to this secluded valley – it's always a couple more turns. Finally you will arrive in the very heart of the Cederberg, sandstone mountains rising all around you in impressive dimensions. You will be given the key to your new home and drive off along half a kilometre of sand track to one of two nothing-short-of-fantastic rustic stone cottages. The river flows past the reeds and rock right by the cottages, clear, deep and wide all year round. You can swim and lie around drying on flat rocks. Birds love it here too. I imagine sitting out on that stoep, on those wooden chairs, looking at that view, beer or wine in hand… a piece of heaven as they say. You can either self-cater, or you can eat at André and Jaen's restaurant back at the lodge. There are a few other cottages nearer the lodge, which are fine, but you must ask for the stone cottages, which are in a league of their own. A pristine slice of unspoiled nature, cherished by a very knowledgeable Marais family who will help with Bushman rock art, horse-riding and fauna and flora. Do not reach for your red pen by the way… that *is* how you spell ceder (in Afrikaans) and that *is* how you spell Jaen!

Rooms: 2 river cottages with 3 bedrooms each.
Price: R360 – R520 for the cottage per night self-catering; or R280 pp for dinner, B&B.
Meals: You can either self-cater or you can eat in the restaurant at Mount Ceder.
Directions: From Ceres follow signs to Prince Alfred hamlet/Op-die-Berg up Gydo Pass past Op-die-Berg. First right signed Cederberge – follow tar for 17 km then straight on on dirt road for another 34 km into a green valley.

Klein Cedarberg

Werner and Vikki Wullschleger
Koue Bokkeveld (Ceres), 6836
Tel: 023-317-0783 Fax: 023-317-0625
Email: info@kleincedarberg.co.za Web: www.kleincedarberg.co.za

The highland nature conservancy of the Koue Bokkeveld is a very special area of South Africa, not yet discovered by most tourists (including Capetonians), despite its proximity to the Mother City. The rolling tablelands and mountains are strewn with fascinating sandstone rock formations and even snow in winter. And right in the middle of all that nature-sculpted rock is Klein Cederberg, the home of Werner and Vikki Wullschleger and their son Nik. (Nik is the mapmaker for this book by the way.) When I last stayed here I was treated to an evening light display that would make Jean-Michel Jarre rethink his next show. A huge sunset, followed by full moon and stars, with a low wall of cloud on one horizon undergoing a frenzied electrical storm. There is a special quality to the air here, because you are nearer the heavens. Guests stay in stone cabins, three have fireplaces and each has its own protected terrace. The small stone houses blend into the surrounding landscape, where nary a man-made object jars the senses. There are ostriches in a field by the house, and a major attraction is Werner's daily Bushman rock art tour. I must make mention also of the fruit trees that surround the house. The grapes and nectarines that I was handed straight from the bough made me realise that I had never eaten fruit before! *Closed July.*

Rooms: 4: all double/twin with en/s shower, separate entrances and private terraces.
Price: R250 – R350 pp sharing. Single supplement R75.
Meals: Full breakfast included. Pre-book dinners when you book – about R55 – R75 a head.
Directions: From Ceres take the R303 through Prince Alfred Hamlet, up the Gydo Pass, through Op-die-Berg. 1st right for 20 km, at end of tarred road, right onto gravel road for 5 km. Right to the house.

Tigertrap Cottages

Jackie Solomon
PO Box 566, Riebeek West, 7306
Tel: 022-461-2289 Fax: 022-461-2335
Email: tigertrap@iafrica.com Web: www.tigertrap.co.za

We called Tigertrap home for four months and by the end had to be crow-barred out of the place, so happily ensconced were we. We could not have landed up anywhere more perfect… hundred-year-old cottages with reed and pole ceilings, stone bathrooms, bedrooms with double doors out to private stoeps and gardens, fridges stocked with all the necessaries, DSTV, fantastico linen and sofas and showers and free-standing baths. Happily intermingled with all this, Jackie and Mike provide a never-ending supply of different goods: good conversation, good humour and overwhelmingly good cheer – the best you'll find. The cottages have steps up to a seventeen-metre, salt-water swimming pool and I did thousands of lengths (well hundreds… well, maybe one thousand) before the old earache set in. You probably don't want to hear about that. Lying on a lounger by the pool on a Saturday afternoon, staring up at the Kasteelberg that looms behind the main house, the line of its craggy summit etched against a reliably blue sky, a wind chime softly blowing in the breeze, the odd squawk from a chicken, a stamp of hungry impatience from the horses in the paddock… such was the scenario for the contentedest hours I have spent in South Africa. So thanks Mike and Jackie for four months of ideal living. We can only pity those whose stay will be measured in mere days.

Rooms: 2 cottages: 1 with 3 bedrooms, all en suite, 2 with bath, 1 with shower; 1 with 2 bedrooms, both en suite, 1 bath and 1 shower.
Price: R370 – R440. No single supplement.
Meals: Full breakfast included. Cottage freezers stocked with home-made dinners.
Directions: Riebeek West is 1 hour north of Cape Town. Ask for directions when booking.

Hunters Retreat Guest Farm

Esther Jordan and Trish Lynch
PO Box 318, Tulbagh, 6820
Tel: 023-230-0582 Fax: 023-230-0057
Email: esther@lando.co.za Web: www.lando.co.za/huntersretreat

I leaned happily against my car while Esther dished out tea for the churchgoers who use Hunters church once a month. What a setting. Pure bands of green and blue as rolling vineland meets berg meets sky. The high-thatched cottages down by the wetlands of the dam have their own patios of perfect peace, disturbed only by flashes of brilliant colour as the red bishops weave their nests in the reeds. There are birds everywhere (egrets, kingfishers and ostriches among them), including a couple of solemn blue cranes that check you out like dogs at the gate. There have been a couple of new additions to the Hunter's scene since the last edition. First there is Trish, now sharing the guest house with Esther and every bit as natural, easy-going and humorous; and a blue crane chick whose parents were a mite protective when we visited and make Trish run a gauntlet to and from her cottage. All the rooms are large, homely and bright with big bathrooms and fridges. There's plenty of space out here, an outdoorsy sort of place, great for animals and kids. Grown-ups can go for walks round the dam and commune with the birds.

Rooms: 7: all doubles/twins with en suite bath and shower.
Price: R175 – R220 pp sharing. Singles R210 – R280.
Meals: Full breakfast included and served until 10.00. There are 5 restaurants in Tulbagh.
Directions: From Cape Town take N1 to exit 47 Wellington/Franschhoek/Klapmuts turn-off, left onto R44 via Wellington. Follow R44 for half an hour to Tulbagh. Straight thro' town, 1.4 km on left.

Bartholomeus Klip Farmhouse

Nic Dupper
Elandsberg Farm, Hermon, 7308
Tel: 022-448-1820 Fax: 022-448-1829
Email: bartholomeus@icon.co.za Web: www.parksgroup.co.za
Cell: 082-564-5663

Heavenly scenery cossets this Victorian homestead in its lush gardens and stands of gum and pine. The wall of the Elandsberg Mountains rises up from the game reserve, reflected in the dammed lake by the house. Here guests can have breakfast on the balcony of the boathouse before heading out for an excursion onto the wheat and sheep farm. You are also taken on late-afternoon game drives to see the zebra, a variety of Cape antelope, buffalo, quaggas (a fascinating experiment to reintroduce an extinct variety of zebra), eagles, flocks of blue crane... and the largest world population of the tiny endangered geometric tortoises. But just to be out in such nature! The spring flowers are spectacular and there are 850 (!) species of plant on the property. Back at the homestead you can cool down in the curious round raised reservoir pool, sit in chairs on the stoep; or, if you have more energy, bike off into the reserve or go on guided walks in the mountains. Staff are very friendly, food is cuisine not tucker (and all included in the price). I recommend splashing out on at least two nights. A great place indeed and very popular so book ahead of yourself if possible. *Closed June*

Rooms: 5: 2 doubles and 3 twins; 5 with bath and shower.
Price: R1980 – R2380 pp sharing. Singles rates on application. Includes meals and game drives.
Meals: Breakfast, early morning tea and 4-course dinner included in price.
Directions: From CT take N1 towards Paarl. Exit 47, left at Stop. Follow Agter-Paarl Rd over 4-ways. L signed Ceres. Follow 30 km, past Malmesbury sign to L. Go next R signed Bo-Hermon. Gravel road for 2 km. Bartholomeus Klip signed to L – 5 km.

Oude Wellington Estate

Rolf and Vanessa Schumacher

Bainskloof Pass Rd, Wellington, 7654
Tel: 021-873-2262 Fax: 021-873-4639
Email: info@kapwein.com Web: www.kapwein.com

There seems to be so much to catch the eye even as you rumble along the 800 metre gravel road to Oude Wellington: vineyards on both sides, pet ostriches peering over a fence, ostentatious peacocks and geese. Rolf and Vanessa are clearly the hospitable types (how else could ostriches find a home on a winery?). The estate was originally conceived as a pineapple farm, as seen in the design of one of the gables and it took Rolf and Vanessa two years to restore the whole estate to its former glory. Four rustic double rooms are in the original farmhouse (built in 1790) with pole beams and white-washed walls; the other two are in the more modern main building (well, 1836), along with the beautiful farm kitchen, snooker room and bar, and a terrace looking out over vineyards, where breakfast is served in the summer. There is a partly-shaded pool off to the side of the main house, a brandy still in the barn, and it is a short walk down to the estate's restaurant, the River Café, which is popular with locals (always a good sign). Guests are also invited to watch wine-making taking place at the right time of year. "We farm and dine and love company" say Rolf and Vanessa in their brochure!

Rooms: 6: all doubles with en suite baths.
Price: R190 – R250 pp sharing.
Meals: Full breakfast included. They have a restaurant on the farm called the River Café.
Directions: 2.5 km out of Wellington on Bainskloof Pass Rd – on right-hand side – follow brown signs to Oude Wellington.

Belair

Janet Plumbly
Suid Agter-Paarl Rd, Paarl,
7624
Tel: 021-863-1504
Fax: 021-863-1602
Email: info@belair.co.za
Cell: 082-572-7062

A straight 300-metre drive up two narrow strips of weathered red brick, past roaming gangs of guinea-fowl and rows of vines, takes you up to Belair, a beautiful guest house on its own farm beneath the round dome of Paarl Mountain. The view from the doorstep (and the garden and pool) across the valley towards Franschhoek and the Groot Drakenstein is spectacular… and it is rather lovely inside too. Steps lead up from a large threshing-circle style driveway into the hallway and open sitting room, which mixes antique furniture with comfy sofas and bookshelves bursting with swashbucklers. Behind is the bright breakfast conservatory, which looks onto a rose-filled garden. There are definitely green fingers at work here. Janet's light but stylish touch is in evidence everywhere at Belair, from the terraced gardens to the bedrooms themselves, each with its own distinct character. My favourite was the 'red' toile room at the end. From the house, it's a short walk up to the dam where bird life abounds among the reeds (look out for buzzards when it all goes quiet), a great spot for a sundowner. For the more energetic, Paarl Mountain Nature Reserve is further up the hill, and there are lots of golf courses nearby. *Cape Town Waterfront is also only 35 minutes away and there are great restaurants in and about Paarl.*

Rooms: 4 doubles with en suite bathrooms. 2 are twins joined together.
Price: R200 – R350 pp sharing. Single supplements not specified.
Meals: Full breakfast included.
Directions: On R101 (Suid Agter-Paarl road) next to Fairview wine estate.

Roggeland Country House

Gordon Minkley
Roggeland Rd, Dal Josaphat Valley, Paarl, 7623
Tel: 021-868-2501 Fax: 021-868-2113
Email: rog@iafrica.com Web: www.roggeland.co.za

The highlight of a stay at Roggeland must be the food! All reports glow with praise: 8-12 different wines to taste pre-dinner, an opportunity to chat to other guests and Gordon himself; then four mouth-watering courses each with a different wine specially chosen to accompany it. Vegetarians will be particularly happy and meals and wines are never repeated during your stay. The house is an 18th-century Cape Dutch homestead with large, thick-walled rooms – sometimes huge – with a variety of original features: beam and reed ceilings, thatch, antique furniture. The dining room, for example, is in an old kitchen with its original grate and cooking implements. Some bedrooms are in the main house and some are separate from it, but none let the side down. Character abounds; floors slope, beams curve and attractive bright-coloured walls are often uneven with age; and there are always fresh flowers and home-made soaps in the rooms. Roggeland is family-run and the atmosphere is friendly and caring as a result. Farmland and mountains surround the property and the Minkleys will organize evening rides on horseback into the foothills. Great hospitality and very good value too. *Children by arrangement. Mountain biking and fishing.*

Rooms: 11: 6 twins, 4 doubles, 1 single. All with en/s bathrooms, 7 with baths and showers, 4 with baths and showers overhead.
Price: R375 – R695 pp sharing. Single supplement in high season R175.
Meals: The highlight here is a 4-course dinner with a different wine at each course and wine-tasting, all included in the price. Full breakfast too.
Directions: Take the N1 north from Cape Town. Leave the N1 at exit 62A, go left over the crossroads and follow signs to Roggeland.

Babylons Toren

Margie and David Louw
Klapmuts Rd, Simondium, 7670
Tel: 021-863-3494 Fax: 021-863-1804
Email: babylon@mweb.co.za

Babylons Toren (the Tower of Babylon) is named after the koppie or rocky hill by the house, thought to resemble a ziggurat by earlier (much earlier – the house was built in about 1700) romantics with a bit of imagination. The property is all that you would hope for from a working Cape Dutch farm. There are the old gabled house, the surrounding outbuildings and vineyards, the backdrop of mountains, the sporadic sound of tractors, many dogs… and Margie has opened up one of the courtyard outbuildings – these were once dairy, butchery, bakery – and created a rustic, but very stylish cottage for guests. The ceiling is of pole beams and cut reeds (the width of the house was apparently dependent on the length of the wagon that carried these beams), walls are thick and whitewashed, and the main bedroom itself is of grand dimensions with high ceilings and a decorative mosquito net over twin beds. You can self-cater or indulge in Margie's healthy breakfasts, which are served under a tree with the Simonsberg Mountain not inconsequential in the corner of your eye as you pour yourself another cup of tea. The large pool in the garden is as much yours as your hosts'. In fact a major reason why Margie has guests at all is to share what Babylons Toren has to offer with new people.

Rooms: 1 cottage: 2 double rooms sharing 1 bathroom with bath. (Self-catering or B&B). One-group booking only.
Price: R180 – R220 pp sharing. Singles R200. Self-catering for two R320, for four people R400.
Meals: Full breakfast included. For other meals, self-catering option or restaurants aplenty in the area.
Directions: From Cape Town take the N1 exit 47, onto R44 towards Stellenbosch. Turn left signed Simondium/Franschhoek. Follow road for 6 km. Babylons Toren is on your right in vineyards.

Résidence Klein Oliphants Hoek

Ingrid and Camil Haas
14 Akademie St, Franschhoek, 7690
Tel: 021-876-2566 Fax: 021-876-2566
Email: info@kleinoliphantshoek.com
Web: www.kleinoliphantshoek.com

Sometimes it all comes together so satisfyingly! Ingrid and Camil opened their first restaurant in a Dutch windmill, at the venerable age of 23, then worked their way across Europe – Turkey, France, Belgium – before moving out to South Africa in 2000 and falling in love (at first sight) with Klein Oliphants Hoek. The building has been reincarnated many times in its hundred and some years, built by an English missionary as a chapel in 1888 and at other times a school and a theatre. I'd only been at the guest house a very brief while before I knew instinctively that no single aspect of the place was going to let the side down. The centrepiece inside is the chapel hall itself, with its high-vaulted ceiling, fireplace and original beams, now the guest sitting room; but there are the bedrooms, the scented garden, the verandah and salt-water pool, the views. The highlight, for me, are Camil's evening meals which mix I'm-at-home-and-these-are-my-friends informality, guests drifting in and out of the kitchen (try doing that in London), with the hautest of haute cuisine, created on (and in) a restored wood-burning stove. All in all, a real treat.

Rooms: 7: 3 twins and 4 doubles; all with en suite showers and baths.
Price: R250 – R450 pp sharing.
Meals: Full breakfast included. Dinner is R170 for 5 courses excluding drinks.
Directions: Akademie St is parallel to the main road in Franschhoek (Huguenot St), two streets up the hill.

Lekkerwijn

Wendy Pickstone

Groot Drakenstein, Franschhoek Road, near Boschendal, 7680
Tel: 021-874-1122 Fax: 021-874-1465
Email: lekkerwijn@new.co.za Web: www.lekkerwijn.com

Lekkerwijn (pronounced Lekkervain) is a 1790s Cape Dutch homestead, with a grand Edwardian extension designed by Sir Herbert Baker. You would probably have to pay to look round if Wendy didn't live there. It positively creaks with family history. You can tell when one family have lived in a grand house for generations – all the furniture, fittings and decoration look so at home. This is not some country house hotel, nor some converted annexe. You share the house fully with Wendy whose family have lived here since the late 19th century – unless of course you would prefer the privacy of the wagon house cottage. My strongest impressions are of the central courtyard with its gallery and cloister, the yellowwood floors and beams and the towering palms planted by Wendy's grandfather, the informal taste of the nursery bedroom, a wonderful breakfast... and Wendy herself, who is full of character and so caring of her guests. *You can self-cater in the wagon house cottage and plans for carriage rides are in the offing. Closed occasionally during June and July.*

Rooms: 4: 3 doubles in the house, 1 with en suite bathroom, 2 with private bath and shower; 1 cottage in the wagon house.
Price: R250 (winter rates) – R500 (summer rates) pp sharing. Singles on request.
Meals: Dinners by prior arrangement.
Directions: On R45 at intersection with R310 from Stellenbosch (after passing Boschendal).

Langverwagt

Janette Le Roux
Langverwagt Rd, Kuilsrivier, 7579
Tel: 021-903-1203
Fax: 021-903-1207
Email: rleroux@iafrica.com
Web: www.lin.co.za/langverwagt
Cell: 082-783-9987

Barely 4 kilometres from the endless 'drive-thrus' of downtown Kuilsrivier is the wonderful and improbable working farm and guest house of Langverwagt. But this is more than just a blessed relief from Cape Town's urban sprawl. The final 500m of the drive up the hill from the main road are along a dirt track, through young shiraz vines and a final flourish of hydrangeas. The old farm (1800) has been restored over the past three years, emerging from a tangle of vegetation to become a place of quirky beauty, with a large sunken garden and a myriad of trees providing plenty of shade. The dozens of enormous antique Spanish pots scattered around the buildings are one of the farm's many idiosyncrasies; the accommodation itself is another. You stay in a converted 18th century slave-house (there are pictures of the last two Langverwagt slaves on the walls) whose thick walls and high, thatched ceilings keep the large rooms cool. The stable-like doors add to the unfussy charm of the place, as do the glass frames on the walls indoors, which highlight sections of the original brickwork. Breakfast is served on a stone patio, which has great views across the suburbs to Table Mountain. Walks around the property are highly recommended, and fishing is possible on the two dams. You will thank me for finding so near Cape Town such a friendly family farm.

Rooms: 4: 2 doubles with en suite bath; 2 doubles with en suite shower.
Price: R200 – R220 pp sharing. Singles R220.
Meals: Breakfast included and served till 10.
Directions: From Cape Town take N2 past the airport. Next left onto R300 over M12. Then leave R300 signed Bellville. Right into Kuilsrivier. After 6 or 7 lights turn left and follow signs to Zevenwacht for 2.5 km. House signed up drive to right.

Muldersvlei Estate

Helen Starke

Muldersvlei Road, Muldersvlei, Stellenbosch, 7607
Tel: 021-884-4433 Fax: 021-884-4324
Email: info@muldersvlei.co.za Web: www.muldersvlei.co.za
Cell: 083-631-2229

Helen's home is a Cape Dutch beauty (1817) – ask for a tour and relish the grand dimensions and original yellowwood beams and Oregon pine floors. Muldersvlei dates back to this time as a farm too, today a mix of fruit and wine (shiraz and pinotage). One of the rooms is actually in the manor house, a treat, while the others are in the Cellars, a converted farm outbuilding with its own kitchen-cum-dining room and sitting room; beds are solid and clothed in linen of high quality. There is a farmhouse feeling to the place with fresh flowers in pretty bunches and a porch at the back of the cottage serves as the perfect breakfast-cum-braai setting: in the background the Simonsberg mountains; in the middle distance a sporadic view of the famous Blue Train and the occasional steam train – perhaps a thrill for trainspotters; and cows wander through wild arum lilies in the foreground. There are oaks in the garden for shade, or a swimming pool for further refrigeration. This is a real farm setting from which to sample the many wines of the Stellenbosch and Franschhoek wine routes, including the farm's very own Starke wines. Helen herself is very relaxed and welcoming and another good reason to come to Muldersvlei. *Wonderful bird life on the farm. Helen will direct you to the best viewing spots or organise a tour with an excellent 'birder'.*

Rooms: 3: In the cottage: 1 double and 1 twin sharing a bathroom; 1 twin en/s bathroom. In the house: 1 double with en/s bathroom.
Price: R250 – R300 pp sharing. Single R300.
Meals: Full breakfast included.
Directions: From Stellenbosch, take the R44 for 8 km (approx.) from last traffic light to turn-off to the left into Muldersvlei Road. Continue for 5 km, crossing the railway line. Muldersvlei is the first farm on the right after the railway line. Well sign-posted.

Natte Valleij

Charlene and Charles Milner
R44 betw' Stellenbosch and Paarl, Stellenbosch, 7600
Tel: 021-875-5171 Fax: 021-875-5475
Email: milner@intekom.co.za Web: www.nattevalleij.co.za

Come and lose yourself in the depths of this wild and fecund garden – or do I mean jungle? Ancient trees such as the rare gingco (the oldest in South Africa, once thought extinct), several 200-year-old oaks, and a wealth of growth besides keep the pool, 'moon gate' and old brandy stills secreted in their midst. Guests stay in the simple B&B room next to the main house, its verandah festooned with grandiflora, and eat a breakfast in this most lovely of Cape Dutch homesteads (pictured above), built in 1775. If the weather's fine then you eat out on the patio under its cooling roof of vine. Or you can take one of the cottages lost down garden paths. Vineyard Cottage (pictured below), with direct access to the swimming pool, is the oldest building on the property, its original 1714 reed ceilings still intact. While Cellar Cottage is the most recent addition at 'Nutty Valley', small, cute, rustic, perfect for couples. Come for great charm, rather than luxury, from house and hosts alike. Walks are in all directions up mountains and into surrounding vineyards. *Local bird-watching tours with Charles are a speciality. Well positioned on the Stellenbosch and Paarl wine routes. Self-catering available in the cottage. Horse-riding for one person at a time can be organised.*

Rooms: 3: 1 B&B room, double with en/s bath; 2 cottages (self-catering or B&B); Cellar Cottage sleeps 2 (+ 2 kid's beds); Vineyard Cottage sleeps 6.
Price: B&B R195 – R230 pp sharing. Rates for the whole cottage per night: Vineyard R450 – R625; Cellar R375 – R425.
Meals: Full breakfast included and served until 9.30 a.m.
Directions: From Cape Town take N1 exit 47. Turn right onto R44. Farm 4 km on left.

Summerwood Guest House

Hilary and Malcolm Forbes
28 Jonkershoek Rd, Stellenbosch, 7600
Tel: 021-887-4112 Fax: 021-887-4239
Email: summerwood@mweb.co.za
Web: www.summerwood.co.za   Cell: 082-539-3575

You notice the huge stinkwood tree first, then the swimming pool (a proper one for swimming in). The smooth, well-tended lawns of the garden seem to beckon the guests, who convene round tables on the terrace in the evening, or take a few hours out from wine and history to brave the sun by day. The house itself was built in 1904 by an Italian architect – light and airy, with pretty 'Italian' windows. All the bedrooms are furnished with a summery feel (lots of yellows) and uncluttered, allowing for much clean wall and floor space. The 'room at the top' has panoramic views of garden and mountain. Hilary and Malcolm take the greatest care that their guests are properly orientated, find the best restaurants (some of the best around are a short walk away, as is the Jonkershoek nature reserve and its mountain trails if you feel like building up an appetite). They clearly revel in the relaxed and friendly atmosphere they have created at Summerwood. *Stellenbosch is only twenty minutes from Cape Town International Airport.*

Rooms: 9: 5 kingsize doubles, 4 twins. All have en suite bathrooms with baths and showers.
Price: From R310 – R500 pp sharing. Singles R470 – R720 (to April 2003).
Meals: Full breakfast included and served until 9.30 am. Restaurants nearby.
Directions: Exit 33 from N2, L to Stellenbosch R310. At T-jct turn R for 2.5 km. Second lights turn R – up Dorp St to pancake roundabout. L into Meul St, next roundabout R into Plein St, becomes v. Riebeeck St. Keep L at fork, house on right.

River Manor Guest House

Johan and Leigh Swanepoel
No.6 The Avenue, Stellenbosch, 7600
Tel: 021-887-9944 Fax: 021-887-9940
Email: rivermanor@adept.co.za Web: www.rivermanor.co.za

Since the first edition of this guide, River Manor has annexed the listed building next door, and it is fair to say that Johan and Leigh have gone from strength to strength as a result. A central Stellenbosch townhouse has become two, and thanks to unwavering Swanepoel enthusiasm and attention to detail, both with their guests and with the decor – the African colonial theme has been successfully carried over to the second, older house – the experience remains a rich one. The new rooms are as large as those in the original house, and also furnished with antiques. Beds and bedding are fit for a king and there are many added comforts such as soft towelling bathrobes and port and sherry trays. Old maps on walls, restored leather suitcases and travellers' trunks complete the effect. With the second house also came another garden, where you will find a small health and beauty spa (massage, steam room and spa) overlooking a second pool, ideal for pampering the weary or the self-indulgent. Breakfast is served at the poolside or in the large conservatory, another new addition to the original building. So guests have plenty of different spaces in which to relax between exploratory walks around town. *Closed last three weeks of June.*

Rooms: 14: from standard (very nice indeed) to luxury (yet nicer). All doubles and twins.
Price: Seasonal from R250 – R795 pp sharing. Singles from R450 – R1200.
Meals: Full breakfast included. Restaurants nearby.
Directions: From CT take the N2 turning to Somerset West. Follow signs to Baden Powell Drive and then to Stellenbosch. On entering Stellenbosch turn right at 2nd set of traffic lights into Dorp St, follow the road all the way to the top, round to the right and take first left which is The Avenue.

Graceland

Sue McNaughton
Stellenrust Rd, Stellenbosch, 7599
Tel: 021-881-3121 Fax: 021-881-3341
Email: pmcm@iafrica.com Web: www.gracelandvineyards.com
Cell: 082-441-2680

Banish Elvis from the mind, because Nashville this ain't. Graceland derives from the three Graces who feature on every bottle of wine the vineyard produces (merlot, shiraz and cab sav)… although Sue's husband Paul happens to be a big fan of the King too, as it goes. They live in a huge thatched house at the end of a long driveway, which opens up at the back onto a large lawn, large garden, large swimming pool, correct-sized tennis court and a small putting green. Beyond this is the cottage, which houses one of the bedrooms, while the other is a secluded gem in the loft. The lawn gradually gives way to the vines and cellars beyond – wine tastings are a must… at 9.30 in the morning in my case. Guests are free to roam the property with walks up through the vines to the Helderberg. In fact Sue is so generous with both her time and the space she gives you that you may experience a moment of distress and disorientation when the time comes to leave. Suddenly it dawns on you that all this is in fact someone else's! But you can at least take some of it away with you – I recommend the Merlot.

Rooms: 2: 1 twin cottage with shower; 1 double with bath.
Price: R200 – R400 pp sharing.
Meals: Full breakfast included.
Directions: Take R44 south out of Stellenbosch for 5 km and it is on the left hand side. 400m along dirt track on right. There is no right-hand turn on R44 from south.

Zandberg Farm

Ernst Heusser
96 Winery Rd, Stellenbosch, 7135
Tel: 021-842-2945 Fax: 021-842-2945
Email: info@zandberg.co.za Web: www.zandberg.co.za

Ernst's model village is a lush oasis. His grapes ripen in blazing sunshine in the surrounding vineyards, but dive into Zandberg, where huge oak trees, stands of bamboo, grassy lawns and a large swimming pool mean cool, green light, water, birds… altogether another world. Guests emerge from their cottages for early evening drinks – they're on the house – and as often as not will go on to dine at the restaurant, 96 Winery Rd, a buzzy and popular eatery by the entrance to the farm. A pleasure to dine in style and then only have to stagger a few yards to your bed. They also do a braai for guests on Sunday evenings – bring your own meat or pay €5 (Euros) a head. The old Cape Dutch barn has a cool interior with pole beams and thick, whitewashed walls hung with Maasai shields and Boer war prints. It's a games room (billiards and table tennis) one end, a sitting-about area the other. Next door the old coach house has become the bar and the next building is the breakfast room where champagne is a daily ritual. Further exploration uncovers an unusual chapel with stunning stained glass, a small village for the staff, a lake, even a patch of jungly bushland. The further I walked the more I liked it.

Rooms: 11 cottages: 7 with bedroom and sitting room; 5 with open-plan bedroom.
Price: €52-55 (Euros!) per person per night.
Meals: Full champagne breakfast included. Free braais on Sunday evening. Every other evening of the week bar drinks are free from 6 – 7 pm.
Directions: From CT take N2 to exit 43. Left onto R44. 6 km then left onto Winery Rd (M6). Number 96 on the right.

Longfield Cottage

Pieter and Nini Bairnsfather Cloete
Eikendal Rd, off R44, Somerset West, 7130
Tel: 021-855-4224 Fax: 021-855-4224
Email: ninicloete@iafrica.com Web: www.longfield.co.za

A gravel road climbs the mountain, escorted on both sides by vineyards. And at the top Longfield House occupies a sensational vantage, gazing out like an Inca on the dramatic Helderberg, and all the way to Cape Point on clear days. Wine is an unavoidable motif in the area generally, but perhaps even more so at Longfield. Pieter's family have been farming in the region since the 17th century, the Eikendal and Longridge wineries surround the property… and didn't we share a sociable bottle over an impeccable salad lunch 'thrown together' by Nini. The Cloetes have restored for their guests an old worker's cottage by the horse paddocks above the house. The country-style sweetness has been retained with whitewashed walls, wicker seats, fir cones in the fireplace, matting floors, stoep and small garden; rustic yes, but very comfortable with it. There's a great big bath with brass taps, a separate shower, telly, and everything in the kitchen you might need to self-cater. The cottage has been left open-plan, a step dividing the sitting and sleeping areas for added light and air. How nice to withdraw up to your private mountain eyrie after a hot day at the wineries, on the beach or perfecting your golf swing. I think most guests just chill out with the view and don't bother.

Rooms: 1 cottage with twin beds and bath and separate shower.
Price: R550 – R650 for the cottage.
Meals: A breakfast basket is provided with yoghurts, fruit, juices, muesli, muffins, wholewheat bread. Also eggs and bacon are provided for you to cook.
Directions: From CT take N2 past the airport, take exit 43 Broadway Bvd. Left at lights. From the next lights 6.3 km exactly, then right into Eikendal Rd. Follow up gravel road, jink left onto tarmac and follow to top and Longfield House.

Manor on the Bay

Hanél and Schalk van Reenen
117 Beach Rd, Gordon's Bay, 7140
Tel: 021-856-3260 Fax: 021-856-3261
Email: manorotb@mweb.co.za Web: www.manoronthebay.co.za
Cell: 082-896-5790

Hanél and Schalk van Reenen are a young couple, and their enthusiasm for the job is palpable. They have poured great vats of time and energy into restoring their property, moving an impressive tonnage of earth to create a raised garden at the front, below a long terrace. This is a great place for watching sunsets over False Bay, or even whales in spring, and the view is conveniently framed by two large palms. A brace of Old English sheepdogs, Yuka and Kayla, complete the very friendly reception committee. Beach Road, you won't need telling, is just next to the sea, and a hop, skip and a dive takes you across the road and into the water. If you don't fancy the walk, however, there's also a pool out the back. Of the seven rooms, four are sea-facing and open onto the terrace, but the other three are just as enticing and luxurious, and look out over a large garden that climbs up the Gordon's Bay hillside. Breakfast is either healthy (in Hanél's case eaten after an early run on the beach – you don't have to join her, so don't worry) or hearty, and is served in the bright dining room or on the terrace outside.

Rooms: 7: 4 doubles and 3 twins all with en suite bathrooms; 4 with sea view, 3 looking on to the garden court.
Price: R320 – R500 pp sharing. Singles plus R150.
Meals: Full breakfast included.
Directions: From Strand on the R44, take Beach Rd turning just before BP garage. From N2 take Sir Lowry's Pass to Gordon's Bay and cross over on to van der Bijl St, down to Beach Rd and L.

Barnacle B&B

Jenny Berrisford

573 Anne Rd, Pringle Bay, 7196
Tel: 028-273-8343 Fax: 028-273-8343
Email: barnacle@maxitec.co.za Web: www.triponline.net/barnacle
Cell: 082-925-7500

Come and explore Jenny's seaside idyll. Several different natural environments collide right outside her cottage. From the deck at the back – with views all the way to Cape Point – you walk down rickety (but safe!) steps to her lawny enclaves in the marsh reeds where narrow paths lead you to the river and beach. The sea is a hundred yards of the whitest, finest sand to your left; beyond the river fynbos and milkwood 'forest' climb the mountain, a nature reserve. You don't have to be a kid to love this. There are otters in the river, baboons on the mountain, estuarine and fynbos birds aplenty... and Jenny is a horticultural expert in one of the world's most amazing natural gardens. Rooms are simple and country cosy, one with a Victorian slipper bath, another with a solid brass bed and the whole place is super relaxed... a hidden gem. *Jenny has canoes and paddle skis to take out on the river. This area has been proclaimed a world biosphere reserve.*

Rooms: 3: outside annexe double with en suite shower; 1 twin with private shower; 1 double en/s 'slipper' bath. Annexe can be self-catering.
Price: R170 – R250 pp sharing. Singles R240 – R300.
Meals: Full breakfast included. Restaurants in Pringle Bay.
Directions: From Cape Town along N2 turn towards Gordon's Bay before Sir Lowry's Pass – follow coast road for 30 km to Pringle Bay turn – follow signs down dirt roads.

Map Number 2

Buçaco Sud

Jean Da Cruz

2609 Clarens Drive, Betty's Bay, 7141
Tel: 028-272-9750 Fax: 028-272-9750
Email: bucaco@hermanus.co.za Web: www.bucacosud.co.za
Cell: 083-514-1015

Everything in this beautiful place has been designed and built by Jean, including the house itself, which sits halfway up a mountain in South Africa's first Biosphere Reserve, a nature lover's paradise with tranquil lakes, stunning beaches, the Harold Porter Botanic Gardens and a penguin colony. Buçaco Sud was once Jean's castle in Spain (or Portugal I should say), now a flight of personal fancy come true. The upstairs sitting room has windows on both sides, and light streams through to mountain views in one direction and sea views in the other. Guest bedrooms are eye-catching, full of startling colours, flowers and eclectic 'stuff' collected by Jean or donated by friends. They all look down over the sea, except 'Shangri-La' at the back – perhaps my favourite – where you can walk straight out through French windows onto the Kogelberg mountain. Local artists' work (for sale) adds even more colour to the vibrant decor. It's not a place for TVs and mobile phones. Genuine care, a sense of humour and enthusiastic hospitality in a house where every detail is home-spun. *Dinners and lunches available at Casitas, Jean's restaurant in Kleinmond.*

Rooms: 5: 4 doubles and 1 twin; 4 with en suite shower, 1 with en suite bath.
Price: R165 – R275 pp sharing. Singles on request.
Meals: Dinners and lunches at Jean's restaurant Casita's. Will cater for weddings.
Directions: Follow R44 from Gordon's Bay along the coast for 30 km, house signed to left in Betty's Bay – 1 hour from Cape Town.

Map Number 2

Beaumont Wine Estate

Jayne Beaumont
Compagnes Drift Farm, PO Box 3, Bot River, 7185
Tel: 028-284-9733 Fax: 028-284-9733
Email: beauwine@netactive.co.za Web: www.beaumont.co.za

Once I had recovered from the delight of meeting Axel, the Beaumonts' respect-inspiring wolf-husky crossbreed, I began to appreciate how successfully they have converted a moribund, nay derelict, vineyard into a thriving, family-run business. The estate, in the middle of tranquil Bot River, produces some 100,000 bottles of wine annually and makes a pinotage for London wine merchants Berry Bros and Rudd's own label. The main house dates from the mid-18th century, an outpost of the Dutch East India company. Guests stay in two late 18th-century cottages that retain many early features. The Pepper Tree, which has also seen service as a wagon shed and school, has wonderful hand-hewn yellowwood beams and stone walls; and the Mill House is even more atmospheric, with curtain rails made from wood found in the river and work surfaces, lintels and window-sills constructed from Oregon pine planks. The effect, as intended, is to echo the history of the original buildings. Outside, you can sit around an old mill stone and admire the antediluvian water wheel, while the willow-shaded jetty on the farm lake offers one of the Western Cape's prettiest settings for weaver birds, sundowners and wheatland views. *Mainly self-catering; breakfast by arrangement.*

Rooms: 2 self-catering cottages. Mill House has 2 bedrooms (plus 2 extra can sleep in living room); Pepper Tree has 1 double (again 2 extras possible).
Price: R125 – R300 pp sharing per night. Singles by arrangement.
Meals: Self-catering but breakfasts by arrangement (R25 – R40).
Directions: From N2 take exit 92 – sign-posted to Bot River. Follow signs to Bot River and Beaumont Wine Estate is signed off to the right-hand side. Map can be faxed.

Wildekrans Country House

Alison Green & Barry Gould
Houw Hoek Valley, Elgin, 7180
Tel: 028-284-9827 Fax: 028-284-9624
Email: wildekrans@kingsley.co.za Web: www.wildekrans.co.za

From the tufts of moss poking out between the old flagstones of the front path I knew that this was my sort of place. The 1811 homestead is raised above its garden, and looks down on lawns, abundant roses, pear orchards, the large swimming pool and old oak trees. The scene is magnificent with the 'wild cliffs' ('wildekrans') of the berg setting the property's limits, rising from a meadow at the back of the garden. Take a stroll beside landscaped watercourses and lily ponds that neighbour the orchards, and you will encounter wonderful, some might think surreal, sculptures that have been positioned with much thought, and I think argument, where they now stand. They add a touch of the unexpected to this magical garden. Finally a rickety bridge – that inspires little in the way of confidence, but is quite safe – crosses a stream and you find yourself at the foot of the steep, forested mountain. A path leads straight up or you can cross a neighbour's land in search of gentler gradients. The bedrooms are charming, each with a four-poster bed, originally parental gifts to Alison and her many sisters, and views out to the garden. There is a large pool, a contemporary art collection and the Wildekrans winery nearby. Evening meals are conveniently to be had in the Houw Hoek Inn bang next door.

Rooms: 4: 3 four-poster doubles in the homestead with en suite bath (one has a shower too); and 1 self-catering cottage.
Price: B&B R195 – R295 pp sharing. Singles R245 – R295 pp sharing. Self-catering R132 – R240 pp sharing.
Meals: Full breakfast included. Dinners from one-course simple country supper (R35 – R55) to three-course (R65 – R85). All meals are self-served.
Directions: On N2 from Cape Town for 1 hour approx., past Grabouw and 12 km further turn left signed Houw Hoek Inn. Through Houw Hoek gate posts (no gate), follow road round to left. Farm on your right.

Map Number 2

Otters Inn

Estelle and Pieter Spaarwater

28 Marine Drive, Vermont, Greater Hermanus, 7201
Tel: 028-316-3167 Fax: 028-316-3764
Email: otters@hermanus.co.za
Web: www.wheretostay.co.za/ottersinn

Estelle and Pieter are hugely enthusiastic about the charms of the Overberg and love talking about its history, environment and potential. From their house (built in 1926 by the Speaker of the South African parliament) near Hermanus you can visit most of the area's 'jewels' within 30 minutes. You can also join Estelle on a twelve-kilometre beach hike to walk off the superb breakfast, which always includes a house speciality such as crêpes filled with crayfish. Those of a less active disposition can, in season, watch whales frolicking right in front of the house. The Spaarwaters can show you a tidal swimming pool, and there is a fynbos garden too with tiny orchids, a natural playground for local birds. The guest house is arranged around a central hall and an enclosed verandah, and the four wood-floored rooms have shutters, mohair rugs, silk duvets and particularly attractive beds. They are bright and fresh in feel and the Spaarwaters have brought great taste to bear. Two have their own sea-facing sitting rooms and two have bigger bathrooms with baths and showers – you choose. They have a swimming pool too and many books (on whales) to read beside it. *Excellent golf nearby. Closed End of May – mid-July.*

Rooms: 4: all doubles/twins; 2 with en suite bath and shower; 2 with en suite shower and private sitting room.
Price: R260 – R370 pp sharing. Single supplement 40%.
Meals: Full breakfast included and served till 9.30 a.m.
Directions: From Cape Town take N2 for 110 km until signed left to Hermanus. Follow R43 until signed right to Vermont/Onrusrivier. Follow this road straight down to the sea. Left at the bottom, house on left.

Windswael Seafront Whale Inn

Thea Claassen

36 Marine Drive, Vermont, Greater Hermanus, 7201
Tel: 028-316-3491 Fax: 028-316-1853
Email: windbb@hermanus.co.za Cell: 082-558-9834
Web: www.hermanus.co.za/accom/windswael

A South African magazine picked the heavy sleeperwood table on rocks yards from a frothing sea as one of the top ten breakfast spots in Africa. Humpbacks and southern right whales sometimes blithely creep into your field of vision and add a touch of the sensational to this daily ritual. The food will make demands on your concentration too and in the whale season you can imagine the happy confusion as freshly-squeezed orange juice, a selection of fresh fruit, sizzling bacon and sausages and creamy eggs battle with magnificent sea-going mammals for your undivided attention. There is much to do from here apart from whale-watching. Great white sharks breed close by, there's walking in the mountains or lounging on local beaches. The brick house is not the most beautiful from the outside, but once through wide sliding doors Thea's inspirations are given free rein – she even wove many of the rugs on show herself. There are Art Deco chairs, wind chimes and mobiles, rough-hewn nude sculptures (the work of Thea's daughter), hanging abalone shells, wildlife paintings. At the back is a brick courtyard, and half-thatched braai where high-spirited barbecued seafood dinners are another speciality. Windswael offers far more than just breakfast. *Excellent golf nearby. Stop press! A new swimming pool overlooking the sea has now been added.*

Rooms: 4: 1 double, 3 twins. All with en/s bathrooms, 1 with bath and 3 with shower.
Price: R300 – R460 pp sharing. R350 – R500 for singles.
Meals: Full breakfast included. Other meals on request.
Directions: Take N2 from CT and follow signs to Hermanus. About 10 km before Hermanus take second Vermont turn-off, signposted to Onrus. Turn R and follow road winding down to seafront. At T-jct turn L into Marine Drive. 3rd house on L.

Map Number 2

Schulphoek Seafront Guesthouse

Petro & Mannes van Zyl

44 Marine Drive, Sandbaai, Greater Hermanus, 7200
Tel: 028-316-2626 Fax: 028-316-2627
Email: schulphoek@hermanus.co.za Web: www.schulphoek.co.za

Waves roll into the bay, five foot high when I visited, and crash against rocks right in front of Schulphoek Seafront Guesthouse. The sitting room has one of the most exciting sea views you could hope for and, naturally, whales steal into Schulphoek Bay during the season for private viewings. The best room, Scallop – I don't think there is any doubt, despite the extremely high standard! – is upstairs, the whole seaward wall an expanse of window with a sliding glass door and parapet. The smells of the sea are powerful. The other rooms, although without sea views, have solid, hand-crafted oak beds and spectacular bathrooms with double sinks, double showers, huge baths… I mean, you will not find better *anywhere*. Not many places in this area feel the need to provide in-house dinners but your hosts are not taking chances on outside eateries. Guests who want to guarantee themselves delicious food stay in and eat at one long table, on chairs made from vintage wine vats. You can choose from an exhaustive cellar of the finest South African wines. Schulphoek is an intimate, state-of-the-art seaside lodge, but still the sort of place where guests socialise with each other, drinks are on an honesty system and meals are all eaten together.

Rooms: 7: all doubles with en suite bathrooms; 2 with shower, 1 with double shower, 2 with bath and shower, 2 with spa bath and shower.
Price: R435 – R610 pp sharing. Single supplement 50%. Incentive rates for extended stays. R5200 for whole guesthouse, max 14 pax, min 3-night stay.
Meals: There is an in-house chef. Full breakfast included. Lunch and dinner on request – advance booking essential.
Directions: R43 into Hermanus from the N2. Take Sandbaai turn-off into Main St. At 3rd 'stop' sign turn left, into 3rd street. Continue to next junction and they are across the road (3 flags).

Blue Gum Country Lodge

Zane and Marian Gibson

PO Box 899, Stanford, 7210
Tel: 028-341-0116 Fax: 028-341-0116
Email: bluegum@kingsley.co.za Web: www.bluegum.co.za
Cell: 082-742-5085

Blue Gum had been open for five months when we visited, but it already had a buzz about it and I expect it's positively humming by now. The setting is beautiful and Zane's enthusiasm rubs off easily. Vines (sauvignon blanc, chardonnay, shiraz) will have been planted on the slope next to the lodge by the time you read this, but otherwise everything is in place and growing fast. The main building houses the restaurant where a multi-gifted Annelize – once an opera singer, now chef and manager! – gives it a distinct Cape flavour… and the menus are as eclectic as she is. There are also a bar and lounge, while the five rooms are across the way. You are accorded much space and comfort, a 'Jetmaster' fireplace and a braai terrace outside. This is hassle-free and dummy-friendly: order one of five different braai menus from the kitchen… just try not to burn it! The main focus here, however, is on the great outdoors, or at least getting a bit of air, so give the brand-new tennis court a go, or borrow a mountain bike and go out for a ride in the hills. If that's not your thing, dig out a bird book and sit on the terrace with a check-list and a glass of wine. *Golf courses, beaches, whale-watching and shark-diving nearby.*

Rooms: 5: 3 doubles with en suite shower and bath; 2 family rooms (1 double and 1 twin) with en suite bath and shower.
Price: R295 – R680 pp sharing. Singles +50%.
Meals: Full breakfast included. Light lunches. Evening meals set menu or à la carte. Traditional Cape cuisine.
Directions: From CT take N2, then R43 turn-off to Hermanus. Drive through Hermanus on R43, following signs to Stanford. At Stanford turn left onto R326 for 6.7 km, then left onto dirt track for 4 km.

Fair Hill Country House

Val and Tim Deverson

R43 between Stanford and Gansbay, Stanford, 7210
Tel: 028-341-0230 Fax: 028-341-0230
Email: fairhill@yebo.co.za
Cell: 082-788-2086

A gate in the middle of nowhere, then a sandy track which leads into the fynbos, arriving finally at Val and Tim's single-story guesthouse. I guarantee that you will be stunned by the quality of natural silence that envelops you as you step from your car. I think you can hear the fynbos growing! Just walk out in any direction and encounter the eland who, Jeeves-like, only materialise when you aren't looking. We stayed here for a weekend break from Cape Town (two hours max) and completely refilled our energy tanks. Walks are lovely down through Fair Hill's fynbos to the beach, which is hard to get to any other way and will most likely be deserted. Those with more momentum can walk all the way to Hermanus and, if she can, Val will pick you up there. Or you can sunbathe by the pool, protected from the wind in the lea of a natural cave. Big rooms are all blessed with verandahs whence to commune with the wilderness. To top it off, the Deversons themselves couldn't be nicer and delicious dinners are part of the (*incredibly* good value) package – with a choice at every course. Fair Hill is an authentic, uplifting and special experience. We recommend you stay for a minimum of two nights. *Self-catering cottage also available.*

Rooms: 6: 5 doubles with en suite bath (and shower attachment). 1 self-catering cottage with bath and shower.
Price: B&B from R250 pp sharing. Dinner B&B from R350. Singles on request.
Meals: All dinners included with choice for each course.
Directions: From Hermanus follow R43 to Stanford – continue past for 8.7 km – electric gates on right. From the Garden Route take R326 after Riviersonderend. At Stanford turn left, continue for 8.7 km, electric gates on the right.

Anlo Guest House

Annelie Rheeder
Guthrie St, De Kelders, Gansbaai, 7220
Tel: 028-384-1201 Fax: 028-384-1201
Email: anlo@kingsley.co.za
Cell: 083-457-8711

Annelie and her sister Ezette will give you a big ol' South African welcome, organise your excursions for you, and cook you delicious meals. The supper I had was as tasty as it was large: soup, bobotie, chicken, pumpkin, a ravishing vinegar pudding, and coffee that's hand-made to their own specifications. The guest house is an involving, upbeat place, many guests excited by their first whale sighting, or great white shark dive. Personally I have no desire to swim in a cage while Nature's greatest killing machine salivates over my love handles, but if that's what lights your candle…. The enormous living room is the heart of the place, with sofas aplenty, rugs, music, books and a large wood-burning stove. You should try to get a room with views of the sea and doors out to the stoep where you can even whale-watch (in season) out in Walker Bay – it's only 150 metres down to the harbour if you want to get closer. Bedrooms are comfortable with many thoughtful extras: after-sun cream, proper bottles of shampoo, make-up remover etc. The new section of the house, guarded by a most convincing talking parrot, is a more ideal place to have meals, freeing up the old dining area as a games room. This is a guest house getting better, not bigger.

Rooms: 5: 1 double with shower and bath, 1 double with shower and 1 twin with bath; 1 twin with shower & bath; 1 family unit.
Price: R260 – R300 pp sharing. Singles +R100. Dinner, B&B R360 pp sharing.
Meals: Full breakfast included. Dinners by arrangement for groups. See above DB&B price.
Directions: Take R44 from Hermanus for about 45 km on road to Gansbaai. Signposted at first sign towards De Kelders. House about 3 km before Gansbaai. Map can be faxed.

Klein Paradijs Country House

Susanne and Michael Fuchs
Pearly Beach, Gansbaai, 7220
Tel: 028-381-9760 Fax: 028-381-9803
Email: kleinparadijs@lando.co.za Web: www.kleinparadijs.co.za

Paradise would be a proud boast, so perhaps Little Paradise is a more defensible claim. But you can see why the name stuck: nature on the one hand, man-made environment on the other, and all rounded off by delicious cooking and green fingers. I'll elaborate. The property stretches up a mountain covered in indigenous fynbos vegetation and nearer the house there is a reed-edged dam with weaver birds, an old camphor tree in the courtyard and an amazing garden whose swimming pool acts as moat to a tiny island of plant life. Inside, high open spaces are punctuated with lovely things: bright paintings, vases of proteas and pincushions, a stinkwood grandfather clock for example. A-shaped rooms have soaring thatched roofs, dormer windows, beams, window-seats, balconies and the curtained-off bathrooms are truly luxurious. The Fuchs are Swiss and have brought many talents with them. Susanne was a translator and speaks English, German and French, while Michael is a chef – they open a small but excellent restaurant in the evenings. *Whale-watching possible nearby from June to November.*

Rooms: 5: 2 twins and 3 doubles; all with en/s bathrooms, 2 with bath and shower, 3 with showers.
Price: R350 – R600 pp sharing. Single supplement +50%.
Meals: Full breakfast included. Lunch and dinner by arrangement. The restaurant is fully licensed.
Directions: From Hermanus take the R43 through Stanford and Gansbaai. Go left at Pearly Beach crossing, then 1st left again. The house is on the right.

Herberg Roosje van de Kaap and Logement

Nick and Ilzebet Oosthuizen
5 Drostdy St, Swellendam, 6740
Tel: 028-514-3001 Fax: 028-514-3001
Email: roosje@dorea.co.za
Cell: 082-380-4086

The Oosthuizens' Herberg is a family affair; Ilzebet runs the guesthouse and is also head chef at their restaurant (where guests have first pick of the tables). Nick, meanwhile, is a lawyer by day, pizza chef by night. The candle-lit restaurant is charming and encourages intimacy – guests often end up chatting to each other across the tables. The menu mixes South African specialities (I had delicious *bobotie*) and international goodies – and pizza of course. Bedrooms in the converted Cape Dutch stables are small and adorable, while those in the Victorian house next door are larger (state your preference). All have shower rooms, some romantically lit by candle only. The feeling is one of an unpretentious country farmhouse with thick whitewashed walls, good solid furniture collected by the Oosthuizens from local fairs and sales, curtains and linen with country flowers, stripes or checks. And there are bunches of wild flowers everywhere you look. Guests can also bask like reptiles in the garden or pool on those hot Swellendam summer days. *Restaurant closes over Christmas and New Year.*

Rooms: 8: all with en suite shower rooms.
Price: From R165 – R200 pp sharing. Singles R250.
Meals: Full breakfast included, dinners available in the restaurant.
Directions: From Cape Town, take the 4th exit off the N2 to Swellendam. Count the turn-off to Swellendam industrial area as the first. After turning off, take the first street left. From the east, after turning off the N2, it's the first street left.

Map Number 3

Kliphoogte

Herman and Marita Linde

Swellendam, 6740
Tel: 028-514-2534 Fax: 028-514-2680
Email: kliphoogte@telkomsa.net Web: www.kliphoogte.co.za

Three kilometres of dusty track bring you to Kliphoogte, one of South Africa's most charming farm B&Bs. Herman, absurdly cheerful for a man who gets up at 4.30 am, runs a fruit and dairy farm on the banks of the Leeurivier… while his mother Marita looks after the guest house. Herman represents the fifth generation of Lindes to work the property, and will take guests on walks around the farm, or leave them in the company of the boisterous weaver-birds to swim at the lake. At meal times, Marita takes charge and cooks typical South African dinners. Bread, butter and milk are all home-made, as is the lemonade and brandy cake. After dinner, Herman will probably sing to you, and then take you in his 4x4 up a nearby hill to look at the stars. The main bedroom is a sweet, blue affair with sturdy old Afrikaner furniture, family photos and rugs made by the farm workers. The other two rooms, which also share a bathroom, are more functional, but this is not a place where you will want to spend long in bed; there is too much going on outside. To sit on the Kliphoogte stoep, listening to the cicadas, and look out over the small, lush valley is to know contentment indeed.

Rooms: 3: 2 doubles and 1 twin; 1 en suite shower, 2 with shared bathroom.
Price: R175 – R250 pp sharing. Single prices on request.
Meals: Full breakfast included. Dinner available, 3 to 4 courses: R100. Lunch and picnics on request.
Directions: Turn off N2 onto R60 (Swellendam turn-off). After 10 km, Kliphoogte (blue sign) is on your left. Then 3 km more on gravel road.

Map Number 3

Jan Harmsgat Country House

Brin and Judi Rebstein
Swellendam, 6740
Tel: 023-616-3407 or 023-616-3311 Fax: 023-616-3201
Email: brinreb@iafrica.com Web: www.jhghouse.com

It was symptomatic of the way I was treated at Jan Harmsgat that on the morning of my departure Brin should drop everything and drive to Swellendam to get a new battery for my ailing car. Throughout my stay he and Judi were charming, entertaining hosts, never more so than when we sat down for a truly excellent supper with all the other guests. Jan Harmsgat is beautiful… the photos do not lie. Dating from the 18th century, it sits, surrounded by fruit trees, on the lower slopes of the Langeberg, near the Breede River. The wonderfully restored farmhouse, with its 25-metre sitting room (a former wine cellar) was once called home by Hermanus Steyn, who proclaimed the independent Republic of Swellendam in 1795. The 680-hectare beef and dairy farm also specialises in almonds, pecans and cheese- and preserve-making… and there are wildebeest and ostriches roaming about too. Guests are housed in old slave quarters whose large rooms and great comfort might make you forget the history of the place. However, sympathetic renovation means that windows in the clay walls have not been enlarged, and the wonky lintels, wooden shutters and vast beams all play their part in preserving the original character here. All is cool and very calm – perfect for hot summer nights.

Rooms: 4: downstairs 1 double with shower and 1 twin with en/s bath; upstairs 1 double and 1 twin each with Victorian baths in the room and an en suite toilet.
Price: R375 (winter) – R650 (summer) pp sharing. Singles R450 – R720.
Meals: Full breakfast included. Dinner is a three-course set menu.
Directions: From Cape Town on N2 to Swellendam; turn onto R60. Carry on for 24.5 km after Swellendam towards Ashton. House on right.

Honeywood Farm

John and Miranda Moodie
Between Swellendam and Heidelberg, Heidelberg, 6665
Tel: 028-722-1823 Fax: 028-722-1839
Email: jmoodie@gardenet.co.za Web: www.honeywoodfarm.co.za
Cell: 083-270-4035

John and Miranda (sweetly known as Mr and Mrs Honey to locals) gave up teaching in Natal and took over the family honey farm in 1989. It's been in family hands since 1817 when the first Moodie left the Orkneys to come to South Africa. The farm is part of a conservancy and borders the Grootvadersbosch Nature Reserve, ideal if you find the call of the wild irresistible. This is one of the richest forests for bird-watching near Cape Town, and when I stayed John took me to see a baby crowned eagle living in one of their own trees. You can also go hiking, horse-riding, mountain-biking (bring your own bikes) and then cool off in a swimming pool fed by a mountain stream. There are four cottages, bedrooms cosily rustic rather than luxurious, with living rooms, open fires and small kitchens. Three of the cottages are set around the central courtyard near the 'Green Room' where Miranda, an artist, serves breakfast and other meals. The fourth cottage, Hunters, is further away and must be one of the most romantic spots in South Africa, tossed in a sea of rolling hills, lit only by hurricane lamps and warmed by a huge open fire. A minimum of two nights is recommended. *A convenient stop-off on the way to Plettenberg Bay and Knysna from Cape Town.*

Rooms: 4 cottages: each with 2 or 3 bedrooms and bathrooms to share.
Price: R150 – R200 pp sharing.
Meals: Full breakfast R30. Dinners R45 – R65 (please book in advance).
Directions: From Cape Town on N2 take the first road to Suurbraak (R324) after Swellendam and continue straight (you will pass the turn to Tradouw's Pass) until you arrive at a dirt road. Carry on straight until you start seeing signs for Honeywood.

Map Number 3

Skeiding Guest Farm

Neels and Anné-Lize Uys

Route N2, Heidelberg, 6665
Tel: 028-722-1891 Fax: 028-722-2223
Email: skeiding@sdm.dorea.co.za
Web: www.whalecoast.co.za/accom/skeiding/ Cell: 082-451-4965

Neels and Anné-Lize are fantastically energetic – you need to be to run a farm, a young family and a guest house in the same lifetime. Guests eat wholesome farm cooking at dinner (all together) and are involved as far as possible in the workings of the farm. This could mean watching the 1500 ostriches being fed in the morning, but there are also indigenous beef cattle, some sheep and goats, two dogs called Asterix and Obelix... and a couple of young children too. The farm is on high, open, rolling terrain, but it is only a short drive into surprising, Garden Route-style forest and the beautiful Grootvadersbosch Nature Reserve for day hikes. The area is a birder's paradise too with 17 endemic species and they have counted at least 50 species on the farm itself. Alternatively, you can head down over South Africa's only working ferry to the De Hoop Nature Reserve or go to Witsand (35 km) for the whales (June to November) and boat rides. It's an outdoorsy sort of place and bedrooms have all you need with strong showers. The cottage rooms have their own sitting area too. A friendly family farm and an education for city slickers. *Professionally run horse rides can be arranged.*

Rooms: 4: all doubles/twins; 1 with en suite bath and shower; 2 with en suite shower; 1 with wheelchair-friendly en suite shower.
Price: R150 – R250 pp sharing. No single supplement.
Meals: Full breakfast included and served when you want it. Dinner R60 – R80.
Directions: From Swellendam take N2 towards Mossel Bay. 45 km after Swellendam (12 km before Heidelberg) farm signed to left. Follow 2 km then signed left again. 3 more km then signed left again. House on hill.

Riversyde

Dora Hattingh
2 Long St, Great Brak River, 6525
Tel: 044-620-3387 Fax: 044-620-3387
Email: riversyd@mweb.co.za Web: www.riversyde.co.za
Cell: 082-784-5885

Dora asked me to fill in a questionnaire about her guest house and I realised then that she had every angle covered – impeccable food, personality, award-winning service, comfort, beds, linen, garden. All got top marks, and not because I was sucking up! There are only four rooms in the house, all large with deep carpets and egg-shell blue or salmon pink walls. One has a little balcony, two overlook the river and two have free-standing iron baths behind screens in the bedroom with you. For some reason I loved this – perhaps because I could watch TV from the bath. You must make sure you book with Dora early enough to give her time to include you in her delicious dinners. But perhaps the most remarkable aspect of Riversyde is the river side. The tidal Great Brak River runs beside the lawns of the garden and there is an island rich in birdlife just a few metres from the jetty. The motorised raft can be taken two kilometres downstream to safe and unspoilt beaches. Or you can fish off it. There are canoes in the house too. Few hostesses take such deserved pride in what they do. *Good base for golf, game viewing, beaches and day-trips to Oudtshoorn, Mossel Bay and George.*

Rooms: 4: all doubles with en suite bath or bath and shower.
Price: R250 – R450 pp sharing. Single supplement 50%.
Meals: Breakfast included and served at any time. Dinners by prior arangement: R100 for 3 courses.
Directions: From Mossel Bay take N2 towards George, signed left into Great Brak River. Follow past 2 stop signs. House on right before bridge.

Susan Pardew Guest House

Toeks Erasmus and Marthie Oberholster
Susan Pardew Rd, Hersham, Great Brak River, 6526
Tel: 044-620-2349 Fax: 044-620-2349
Email: susanpardew@intekom.co.za Web: www.guesthousesusanpardew.co.z
Cell: 082-782-8975 or 082-380-0567

If you're after a beachy time then you might as well do it properly. At the Susan Pardew Gues
House the surf crashes continually below you and the views and salty breezes of the beach
permeate every corner of the place. Obviously the big deck is a major draw and I found myself
wrestling the catch of the door to get out there before I'd even said hello to Toeks and Marthie
The big deck, which leads directly onto the dunes and fynbos and down to the beach, is also the
venue for breakfast and there is a plunge pool encased within it too. You are treated to both
sunrise and sunset from here and Mossel Bay glimmers most appealingly at night. Dolphins are a
common sight, as are whales in season. The bedrooms are all very large, with unusual modern
furniture, the two rooms upstairs more like apartments with sitting areas, microwave and fridge
DSTV, hob and sink. The upstairs verandah is shared by both rooms, but all the rooms in the
house have fantastic views of the ocean. Toeks and Marthie do dinners for guests or there's an
indoor braai installed. The Susan Pardew by the way was a ship that was wrecked here in 1872..
in case you were expecting her to bring the tea in the morning.

Rooms: 5: 1 double with en suite bath and shower;
2 twins en/s shower; 2 twins en/s bath and shower.
Price: R150 – R370 pp sharing. Singles R200 –
R450.
Meals: Full breakfast included. Dinners by pre-
arrangement R75 for 3 courses (including wine).
Directions: From Cape Town take N2 past Mossel
Bay. 20 km further turn off onto Great Brak River
ramp. 1st right, under road, left at T-junction. Over
bridge, turn right signed Glentana. 1 km turn right
into Hersham Drive. Keep straight to the end.

Fairview

Philda Benkenstein
36 Stander St, George, 6530
Tel: 044-874-7781 Fax: 044-874-7781
Email: benkenstein@mweb.co.za
Web: www.wheretostay.co.za/fairview

This picturesque, listed Victorian house on the eastern edge of George is an intriguing place to stay. With its high ceilings and abundant Victoriana, Fairview has the feel of an old English rectory, although the vivid colours owe more to African than Anglican themes. The bedrooms are a treat, particularly the two in the main house, which still have their original 1880s floorboards, beams and fireplaces. The Orange Room, complete with dashing white trim, bathes in afternoon sunlight, while the Yellow Room soaks up the morning. If you're lucky, you'll be able to choose between them on arrival. The sitting room has the same high ceilings and wooden floors, with shuttered sash windows and enormous linen press. The Benkensteins have retained many of the original window-panes… a hindrance to their sons' cricketing exploits perhaps, but they add to the authenticity of the restoration. Philda used to be a nurse but is far happier running a guest house. She loves having people in the home and will happily cook South African meals if people want them. Husband Desmond, a green-fingered doctor, is the creative force behind the glorious garden – *nota* particularly *bene* the rhododendrons and orange trees.

Rooms: 3: all doubles with extra bed possible; 2 with en suite shower, 1 with en suite bath. One is a self-catering flat.
Price: R200 – R240 pp sharing. Singles R240 – R280. Self-catering rates on request.
Meals: Full breakfast included. Dinners by request. Philda is a keen cook specialising in SA dishes.
Directions: From CT on N2 take York St turn-off to George. Turn right at T-jct into Courtenay St. Over railway bridge and turn left into Second Street and turn left at stop sign into Stander St, house on right.

Somanga Country Lodge

Andrew and Jenny Tainton
PO Box 9959, George, 6530
Tel: 044-881-0090 Fax: 044-881-0083
Email: somanga@iafrica.com Web: www.somanga.com

It was hot when I arrived at Somanga (my pen had just melted in the February heat!), but I was soon cooled and calmed by the peace and stillness of this remarkable place, whose name means 'unexpected surprise' in Xhosa. New A-framed pine chalets (à la Swiss Alps) line up along an escarpment, each with its own balcony with stunning views over the mountains and all the way to Mossel Bay on the coast. Each chalet has big double doors onto the balcony, bright covers on beds and sofas, wicker seats and discreet TV. Jenny and Andrew have also built a central breakfast-cum-dining area as they find many of their guests prefer to eat chez Somanga rather than schlep into town if they've had a long drive. There are 73 hectares in all and the farm grows grenadillas and clementines. The drive and gardens are full of flowers (400 rose bushes) and recently planted indigenous fynbos plants. And then at the other end of the property is forestry into which you can ride or walk directly from Somanga. Birds, of course, love gardens, forests and fruit farms. Jenny and Andrew, not satisfied that you will be fully occupied with all this, have also laid out a swimming pool, a pitch and putt course on which to practise your golf swing (golfing groups are catered for) and cut hiking trails in the forest. You don't *have* to do anything of course.

Rooms: 6 chalet doubles with en suite bath or bath and shower. Also 4 self-catering units sleeping max. 4 people per chalet.
Price: R375 – R475. Singles R565 – R715. Self-catering: 2 pax R425, 3 pax R345, 4 pax R305 etc. Specials and golfing groups available.
Meals: Full breakfast included and served till 10 a.m. Dinners, lunches and picnic hampers by prior arangement about R35 – R120.
Directions: From Mossel Bay take N2 towards Knysna. Left signed George airport. At crossroads (R102) go straight over and turn left signed Somanga. Next right signed Somanga again. Follow road for 5 km until dirt road signed right to Somanga (Koesterbos Rd).

Strawberry Hill Country Lodge

Lynda Turner
Old George – Knysna Rd (Seven Passes Rd), George East, 6530
Tel: 044-877-0055 Fax: 044-877-0226
Email: getaway@strawberryhill.co.za
Web: www.strawberryhill.co.za

The Turners must love watching the reaction of their guests as they first confront the view at Strawberry Hill. I started applauding, congratulating people and ordering copies of the prints! The valley plunges straight from the lawns in front of the house and nothing spoils the unfettered natural beauty of this hill-marooned farm. Lynda had commandeered Bill (her father-in-law) to lead me down the mountain trails through ferny afro-montane forests to 'The Point', a hidden idyll of cascading water at the frothy confluence of two rivers. We went for a swim in the rock pools and guests are ordered (by me!) to take a picnic on a fine day and explore. Back at the lodge fastidious attention to detail sees luxury piled on luxury. Huge baths with lots of water pressure, separate showers, soaps and shampoos, wonderful linen on new beds, mohair blankets. Drinks and dinner are taken with the other guests (before a log fire on cool nights) – delicious crudités, tomato soup and Malay curry on the night I stayed. Breakfast was equally hard to fault – typically I was given a whole jug of freshly squeezed OJ. Strawberry Hill bowled me over because it is so rare for a place to provide such extremely high levels of comfort without compromising one smidgin on the friendly family atmosphere.

Rooms: 5: 1 suite (balcony, sitting room and shower – sleeps 2 extra on divan); 1 twin/king with corner bath and shower; 1 double. (2 new rooms due by August.)
Price: R200 – R450 pp sharing. Singles +50%.
Meals: Full breakfast included. Dinners also available on request: R110 – R125 excluding drinks.
Directions: Faxed or emailed on request.

Hilltop Country Lodge

Magda and Hennie Schoeman
Victoria Bay, George
Tel: 044-889-0142 Fax: 044-889-0151
Email: welcome@hilltopcountrylodge.co.za
Web: www.hilltopcountrylodge.co.za

Approach along a narrow sealed road and you eventually emerge on an open hilltop, catching exciting taster-glimpses of the view through the windows and doors of the house. You will be shown to the front patio and there, hundreds of metres below, the 40-kilometre sweep of Wilderness Beach arcs away, while in the foreground neatly tended and well-watered flower gardens, clucking with hens and their chicks, run down into the plunging fynbos. The swimming pool, teetering on the edge of the mountain, offers perhaps the best sensation of height of all. Hennie's family have owned this dramatic parcel of land since the 1960s, and they used to come and holiday here before the lodge was built. Their bit of mountain has now been designated a private nature reserve, so no new buildings will ever spoil the party. The bedrooms today are very luxurious. All have private entrances and balconies with the view, mohair rugs on beds for cool nights, lampshades made of twine and many of the antiques were collected by the Schoemans in Japan. Most guests will spend their days on the beaches (Wilderness or Victoria Bay) or exploring the forested hinterland of the Garden Route. But there are plenty of reasons to spend at least one full day lounging around at Hilltop. *Some restaurants in the area do a pick-up service.*

Rooms: 6: 4 doubles, 2 twins/doubles. 4 rooms have en/s baths, 1 has en/s jacuzzi and shower, 1 has shower. All have seaviews except one!
Price: R400 – R750 pp sharing. Singles +50%.
Meals: Full breakfast included and served until 10. Lots of restaurants locally.
Directions: Take Victoria Bay turn-off off N2. After 800 metres Hilltop is signed off to the left.

Land's End

Rod and Shanell Hossack

The Point, Victoria Bay, George, 6530
Tel: 044-889-0123 Fax: 044-889-0141
Email: landsend@worldonline.co.za or LandsEnd@vicbay.com
Web: http://vicbay.com

Sea, surf, sun, salt, sand, sleep... Land's End was a dilapidated old Victorian holiday cottage when Rod and Shanell bought it. It is now utterly transformed. The downstairs remains Victorian in character while the upstairs part of the house is new and nautical, with a blue wooden deck and whitewashed walls. Decoration in all the rooms is modern with colourful bed covers from Mexico and Indonesia for a splash of ethnic chic. Guest rooms downstairs are centred around a sitting and dining room with shelves of books and cosy-looking armchairs that grab and don't let go, while upstairs there is a suitably private 'honeymoon' suite. But all the rooms have to face the amazing fact of the sea right there, almost within touching distance – the perfect lullaby. Rod has travelled the world with his surfboard, but it is difficult to conceive of a more perfect place than Victoria Bay for a born-to-surf South African to raise a young family. Among its attractions are a famous surfing wave, a good look-out point for passing whales and a view of the Outeniqua Choo-Tjoe every afternoon. Rod has also taken out membership of Fancourt Country Club, a great golf course, on behalf of his guests.

Rooms: 6: 4 doubles and 2 twin rooms that adjoin 2 of the doubles for families. All en suite bathrooms.
Price: From R200 – R450 pp sharing. Singles from R350 – R450.
Meals: Full breakfast included served until anytime. Light lunches and sandwiches provided by prior arrangement.
Directions: Midway between George and Wilderness, signed on N2 to Victoria Bay. Either phone or walk to Land's End to collect keys to get through gate.

Map Number 3

The Waves

Liza and Iain Campbell

7 Beach Rd, Victoria Bay, George, 6530
Tel: 044-889-0166 Fax: 044-889-0166
Email: thewaves@intekom.co.za
Web: www.gardenroute.co.za/vbay/waves/index.htm

Iain and Liza have an amazing photo from 1906 when The Waves was the only house on the beach, used as a holiday home by an Oudtshoorn farmer. It is not surprising a few others have since joined the club. The hamlet is closed to vehicles – only residents hold the key to the gate, so you can park your car securely at night. I'm no surfer, but the waves here are enticing, rolling up the perfect arc of this small bay at a height that is challenging, but not scary. Iain will give you a wetsuit and surfboard, or fins and a snorkel. Or, if you like your activity less damp, there is horse riding nearby or three lovely walks of handy lengths – one, two or three hours. The house is right on the sea (see above) and all three bedroom suites (each has its own lounge) look out, although you may spend more time on the verandah watching the waves roll in. They are hypnotic. Whales (in season) may heave into sight to your right, while to your left the Outeniqua Choo Tjoe (yes, it's a steam train) runs through Victoria Bay twice a day. Iain and Liza are consummate hosts and great fun. Bay life could be addictive.

Rooms: 3: doubles with extra beds; 1 with en suite shower, 2 with en suite bath and shower.
Price: R275 – R450 pp sharing. Singles R375 – R550.
Meals: Full breakfast included and served till 10 a.m.
Directions: From Mossel Bay on N2 past George exits where highways merge. 1 km signed Victoria Bay to right – follow down hill 3 km. Park and walk along beach road to collect the key for the gate.

Kingfisher Country House

Phil and Sue Millard
1030 Dumbleton Rd, Wilderness, 6560
Tel: 044-877-1955 Fax: 044-877-1955
Email: info@kingfish.co.za Web: www.kingfish.co.za
Cell: 082-808-4379

As Kipling (almost) wrote, if you can keep your head when all around are losing theirs, you're probably Sue Millard. While I was at Kingfisher she had to deal with three new guests and their bad-tempered guide, a pestering me, pouring rain, a (rare) day-long power cut, no telephone…. Sue was an island of calm. Her mood is doubtless helped by the serenity of the environment that she and Phil have created for themselves and their guests. Kingfisher looks out over the Wilderness National Park, a haven for bird-life, canoeists and hikers, while inside, the house has developed a wonderful lived-in feel after just four years. The huge fireplace in the sitting room has an aged, smoke-blackened hearth, the sofas are covered in cushions and mohair rugs, and you may even spot one or two books written by Sue, an expert on traditional country crafts. The bedrooms also show off her fine taste, with two-tone walls, stencilling, dried flowers, lace, cotton drapes, wicker, brass or bamboo beds and headboards and pretty bathrooms. Breakfast on the verandah is a special treat because you can watch the steam-driven Outeniqua Choo-Tjoe (pronounced 'choo-choo') gliding by at the bottom of their beautiful garden. And should you ever want to leave, Kingfisher has a siding nearby so guests can put out their arm to stop the train and climb on board! *Closed normally in June.*

Rooms: 4: all king-size beds convertible to twins; 3 with en suite shower, 1 with en/s bath.
Price: R170 – R260 pp sharing. Singles + 50%.
Meals: Full breakfast included.
Directions: Faxed on booking.

Moontide Guest House

Maureen Mansfield
Southside Rd, Wilderness, 6560
Tel: 044-877-0361
Fax: 044-877-0124
Email: moontide@intekom.co.za
Web: www. moontide.co.za

It's a rare pleasure for us to stay somewhere on *holiday* and to experience it over a period of days. And Moontide was a palpable hit with all five of us. Its position is hard to beat, right on the banks of the lagoon, its wooden decks shaded by a 400-year-old milkwood tree. Here you can sit out for bountiful breakfasts or with an evening drink from your bar fridge, and watch giant kingfishers diving for fish – well, we saw one anyway. Birdlife is profuse on the lagoon. The long, white-sanded Wilderness beach is only a one minute walk from the house, but you can also take a canoe straight from Moontide up the lagoon into the Touw River and then walk up along forest trails to the waterfalls to swim in fresh-water rock pools. Whatever we did it was a pleasure to return, play cards in a relaxed sitting room, or read in the cool of your bedroom. I was delighted with 'Milkwood' because I'm a sucker for dozing on a futon, in a loft, under thatched eaves, with river views by my head. But I would like to return and try them all out one by one. The Boathouse has a private verandah near the water's edge for example. One German guest came to stay and only left once Maureen had agreed to be his wife!

Rooms: 5: 1 'luxury suite' (king & 2 twins); rondavel double with bath & shower; 1 duplex in house (double and 2 singles); stone cottage with twins and shower. The boathouse; twin beds with shower.
Price: R200 – R400 pp sharing per night. Single rates on request.
Meals: Full breakfast included.
Directions: From George on N2 ignore Wilderness turn-off. Cross Touw River bridge, first left signed Southside Rd. Moontide at the end of cul-de-sac.

Map Number 3

Seodin

Marion Britz

373 Waterside Rd, Wilderness, 6560
Tel: 044-877-0554 Fax: 044-877-0554
Email: seodin@intekom.co.za
Web: www.wildernessinfo.co.za/seodin.htm

When Marion was young she had the strange dream of one day becoming a 'seaside landlady in a thatched house' (and I quote). Well, what do you know...! Seodin is not some grand guest house. It's a family home, a proper B&B where the personality of the thatched house and its owner create their own laid-back and unfussy atmosphere. Therefore it's a great place for kids – just two minutes walk from the garden gate, past the lagoon to the beach and one of the bedrooms has fun bunk beds. Both bedrooms are surprisingly large with high thatched ceilings, their own sitting area and each has a kitchenette for those who want to cook their own meals. Guests are hardly expected to take to their rooms like invalids, however, and Marion and her dogs share their house completely with you. If it should rain I can think of nowhere better to be than playing scrabble or cards in the sitting room. It's definitely a happy house. *Wilderness is basically a village in the middle of a national park – where there are excellent walks, adventure trips and riding. A good centre for exploring the surrounding villages and beaches too.*

Rooms: 2: 1 double and 1 family, both with en suite bath. There is one extra shower.
Price: R175 – R220 pp sharing. No single supplement.
Meals: Full breakfast included and Marion is flexible about times.
Directions: From N2 between George and Sedgefield turn at 1st Wilderness sign to left. Follow road round common then left into Limberlost Lane. Seodin on right.

Map Number 3

79

Garden Route, Western Cape

The Gallery Guest House

Lolly Hahn-Page
10 Hill St West, Knysna, 6570
Tel: 044-382-2510 Fax: 044-382-5212
Email: gallery.guesthouse@pixie.co.za
Web: www.galleryguesthouse.co.za   Cell: 083-309-3920

Lolly manages the happy trick of combining her work as an artist with running a friendly, laid-back guest house in a peaceful part of Knysna. She is a strong force for the promotion of arts and crafts in the town – itself a honeypot for those that can hold a pencil steady. Thus 'The Gallery'. Her own and local artists' paintings and sculptures dot the walls and cover the carpets in the guest house, one of the longest-running in Knysna. There is a separate private studio where Lolly desperately tries to find time to 'work'. The main room where breakfast etc happens is upstairs and the adjoining wooden deck has tremendous views out over the Knysna Heads, Leisure Isle and Pledge Park nature reserve. There is lots to do in town, what with sunset boat rides, the Outeniqua Choo-Tjoe, sea swimming, canoeing etc – and Lolly is very knowledgeable. Best of all she has special private places – sunset spots, music venues, beaches, walks and restaurants – you will only find with her help. The bedrooms themselves are simple, showcasing more local artwork, but cater for all your needs. Choose the Gallery for the irrepressible personality of both house and hostess. *Nine good restaurants within 2 mins.*

Rooms: 4: 2 twins and 2 doubles; 1 with private bath; 3 with en suite bath or shower.
Price: R200 – R450 pp sharing. Single rates on request.
Meals: Full breakfast included and served from 8 to 10 a.m.
Directions: From George take N2 to Knysna, 2nd lights turn left into Grey St, then 2nd left into Hill St West, to end of cul-de-sac. Map on web site.

Spring Tide Charters

Stephan and Evelyn Pepler

34 South Jetty, Knysna Quays, Waterfront Drive, Knysna, 6600
Tel: 044-533-4006 Fax: 044-533-4006
Email: info@springtide.co.za Web: www.springtide.co.za
Cell: 082-470-6022

As I took the helm on board the Outeniqua, fifty feet of shimmering beauty somehow under my command, and took her across Knysna lagoon at a leisurely six knots, I felt very special indeed. I was discombobulated no doubt by a heady combination of the yacht, the setting and my own skipperly delusions. The Outeniqua is owned and sailed (often out at sea, weather permitting) every day by Stephan and Evelyn Peplar, a young couple who clearly love what they do and it's not hard to see why. The coastline around Knysna is beautiful and the vessel truly exceptional, and I'm not just saying that because Stephan spent four and a half years building and fitting her out! Every immaculate thing on board, bar the hull, is his own work. The day starts with a call through to the harbourmaster to raise the bridge by the moorings, and you head off across the lagoon to the Heads, a narrow, steep-sided channel that leads out to the open sea and a whole world of excitement. But don't worry… Stephan will always go at your pace, even if the dolphins swimming past you are not. Evenings are spent moored at Featherbed, the calmest part of the lagoon, where Evelyn conjures a quite magnificent dinner from the galley. A wonderful experience.

Rooms: I cabin or family – ideally just a couple can be accommodated. Day, breakfast and sunset trips also available.
Price: Overnight charters from R1450 pp. Day sail and short trip prices start at R250 pp.
Meals: Full breakfast included. Dinner also included.
Directions: Knysna Quay Marina is on the Waterfront Drive. Park on the waterfront, next to the station.

Glenshee

David and Fiona Ramsay

Eastford Downs, Eastford
Nature Reserve, Welbedacht
Lane, Knysna, 6570
Tel: 044-382-3202
Fax: 044-382-3202
Email:
glenshee@mweb.co.za
Web:
www.gosouth.co.za/glenshee
Cell: 082-789-5062

David and Fiona were the first to build up here on the mountain, their pink-washed home blessed (not by chance) with majestic valley views down the steep sides of the Eastford Nature Reserve to the curve of the Knysna River far below. Views they couldn't resist sharing with others… which is where you come in. They built the house themselves, the hundred-year-old windows and doors salvaged from Karoo farms, and the wide wooden deck has become the irresistible focal point of the house. And now they have built a black fibre-glass plunge pool too, further inducement to spend at least one lazy day at Glenshee. The three bedrooms are fresh, light, airy and countrified with wicker bedsteads, excellent linen, your own private deck and viewpoint. David and Fiona really enjoy their guests and operate in traditional B&B fashion, offering much expert advice, over sundowners or tea, on secret spots they have found all along the Garden Route. Or they will point out the best walks from the house through the forests and fynbos. Fiona spends at least an hour each morning preparing the breakfast (Health, Continental or English) and these are taken on the deck with the invigorating view as backdrop. A real home and delightful hosts.

Rooms: 3: 1 double with en/s bath; 1 twin with en/s shower; 1 double/twin with en/s bath and shower.
Price: R150 – R300 pp sharing. Singles R200 – R300.
Meals: Health, Continental or English breakfast included.
Directions: From George, before Knysna, turn left into Welbedacht Lane, go straight for 2 km to crossroads. Go right signed Eastford Downs follow for 250 metres then straight through gates at Eastford Downs. Glenshee is 800 metres down on the left.

Map Number 4

Narnia Farm Guest House

Richard and Stella Sohn

off Welbedacht Lane, Knysna, 6570
Tel: 044-382-1334 Fax: 044-382-2881
Email: narnia@pixie.co.za Web: www.narnia.co.za
Cell: 083-325-2581

Narnia combines just about every element we search for in a place to stay. It's defiantly itself – the style (luxuriously ethnic, but never overdone) is so unusual and so genuine that you know it is the extension of real people, not some pretentious interior design job. Stella (graphic design graduate, protea farmer, mother of two) is one of those people and Richard (lawyer, 'architect' and father of four) the other. Narnia is entirely their creation, a dream slotted round one or two key requirements: the house should have a deck with a clear view to the Knysna Heads; and there should be a big, open, friendly entrance hall. Otherwise the house has grown organically into some mad ship with wooden decks, gangways and staircases, swing chairs, heavenly colours of tropical brilliance ("In a previous life I must have been a Mexican," says Stella), a prize-winning garden, long views in all directions, and smaller surprises everywhere. They are great ones for inventively recycling stuff that you or I might throw away. Stella and Richard amaze me with their great energy and skill with people, despite holding down so many jobs. Go and visit before everyone else discovers it. *Bushbuck are often spotted by the dam on the farm.*

Rooms: 4: 2 doubles with en-suite bathrooms, 1 cottage with 1 twin and 1 double with shared bathroom (self-catering or B&B).
Price: From R245 – R330 pp sharing. Single rates on request.
Meals: Full breakfast included and served from 8 – 9.30am.
Directions: On N2 from George turn in Welbedacht Lane just before Knysna. Then follow signs to Narnia Farm Guest House.

Inyathi Guest Lodges

Ypie Kingma and Erik Ekkelkamp
52 Main Street, Knysna, 6570
Tel: 044-382-7768 Fax: 044-382-7768
Email: inyathi-sa@mweb.co.za Web: www.inyathi-sa.com

I was reminded of an adventure playground of my youth when I did the tour at Inyathi. There was the same inventive use of wood and love of hiding places and alcoves. Every room puts its limited space to work with great humour and ingenuity: some have their own small verandahs, some free-standing baths; there are painted dolphins, bird-of-paradise flowers, stained glass windows, brightly coloured African dolls made of beads, wooden candles, low beds on raised platforms, dried tumbleweed, wicker baskets... and anything else that could be found and put to effective use. All the bathrooms have something quirky about them but number 8 takes the biscuit. You creep downstairs into a dungeon/shower room with black and white diamond walls, hanging wattle stick screens, a row of black wooden carved figures on an exposed wall and a tree growing behind glass as if in a display case. This same tree grows up through the deck and provides shade for the room above. Ypie and Erik are a young Dutch couple who, after six years in Moscow, are obviously still looking for excitement. Very youthful, quirky, friendly and good fun

Rooms: 11: 10 doubles and 1 twin; 7 with en suite bath and 4 with shower.
Price: R160 – R295 pp sharing. Singles supplement +R50 – R75.
Meals: Full breakfast included and served till 10. Braais by arrangement.
Directions: From George or Cape Town, Inyathi is on the left about 400 metres after the first traffic light driving into Knysna on the N2. Coming from Plettenberg Bay, Inyathi is on the right after McDonalds on the left.

Lindsay Castle

Vic and Lea Shewan

Noetzie, Knysna, 6570
Tel: 044-375-0100 Fax: 044-382-0877
Email: reservations@knysnacastles.co.za
Web: www.knysnacastles.com

An extraordinary modern-day turretted castle on the beach. Just outside Knysna you turn down a road signed to Noetzie; this is the border of the Sinclair Nature Reserve and the drive will take you through forest and almost certainly past baboons. At the end of this road, and quite literally on the beach (if the tide is high Vic has to come and fetch you in his 4x4), is Lindsay Castle with its airy, stone interior, terracotta tiles and blue and white fabrics – all strictly in tune with the surrounding, pounding sea. Marine life proliferates! Whales and dolphins cavort (in season) and there are otters, bushbuck and the rare oyster-catcher. You can hike, fish and swim in the estuary or sea and if you crave a glimpse of town-life, holiday-making Knysna is only a 20-minute drive away. At night the sky, undimmed by city neon, is spectacular. Dinners in the castle are a must and a high point of your stay, around a large table made of railway sleepers, with mussels fresh from the rocks or with fresh oysters – Knysna is famous for its oysters – followed by other delicacies from Lea's kitchen. The sound of the sea lulls you to sleep, and heavenly slumbers they are too! *Closed mid-December to mid-January.*

Rooms: 4: all doubles, all with en/s bathrooms (two are in the turrets, one is a honeymoon suite).
Price: R550 – R900 pp sharing.
Meals: Full breakfast included. Lunches and dinners by arrangement (approx R150 for dinner).
Directions: From Knysna, go through the town towards Plettenberg Bay and turn right after approx. 4 km at sign for Noetzie. Follow the road for 5 km until you arrive at the castle.

Lairds Lodge Country Estate

Alison and Murray Brebner
Off N2 Highway, PO Box 657, Plettenberg Bay, 6600
Tel: 044-532-7721 Fax: 044-532-7671
Email: info@lairdslodge.co.za Web: www.lairdslodge.co.za

Alison and Murray are by nature black belts in the hosting arts and have created an intimate, country-house experience for gourmets, in a great location and with sumptuous bedrooms. They take their hospitality (and cooking) seriously here and every guest is treated as special. It's an involving place too, guests coming together in the evening for drinks in the drawing room and then eating together round one table. (This is not an obligatory part of the stay, but highly recommended, especially if you are staying more than one night.) These dinners, based round speciality seafood and venison dishes, are the highlight at Lairds Lodge. Eight of the lodge's ten rooms are in the main house, while two separate garden suites, complete with their own sitting areas, are a more recent addition – all are very large with high ceilings. The Brebners' Cape Dutch homestead sits well in its immediate surroundings, a 24-acre property with plenty of space for appetite-building walks. You can also sit on the terrace, or in the pool, and simply admire the view across to the mountains. Plettenberg Bay's beaches and Knysna's lagoon are also only a short drive away.

Rooms: 10: 2 standard queen-size doubles with en/s shower; 6 deluxe rooms (2 kings & 4 twins) with en/s bath & shower; 2 garden suites (1 king and twin) en/s b & sh.
Price: R350 – R650 pp sharing. Singles + 50%.
Meals: Full breakfast included. 3-course gourmet dinners available most evenings from R130 pp.
Directions: You'll see the sign directing you just off the N2 highway, 8 km from Plettenberg Bay, 23 km from Knysna.

Map Number 4

Southern Cross Beach House

Sue and Neill Ovenstone

1 Capricorn Lane, Solar Beach, Plettenberg Bay, 6600
Tel: 044-533-3868 Fax: 044-533-3866
Email: southerncross@robbergbeach.co.za
Web: www.southerncrossbeach.co.za   Cell: 082-490-0876

… and relax. With this dreamy, whitewashed, wooden house at the quiet end of Robberg beach's long arc, it is impossible not to. Plettenberg Bay is a lively town, with lots of restaurants and bars, but people really come here for the sea, and you would seriously struggle to get closer to it than at Southern Cross. During the Christmas holidays the beach is packed, but for the rest of the year there are more signs of life in the sea. Dolphins race by all year round, revelling in their position at the head of the food chain, with southern right whales often wallowing just in front of the house from June to November. The house itself is just up a wooden gangway from the beach. Wood predominates, with blues and white echoing the ocean. The brochure says 'plantation style', but I would plump for classic Massachussetts beach house. Wooden decking looks across the bay to the Tsitsikamma Mountains to the left and the Robberg Peninsula opposite, which is geologically identical to the Falklands, bizarrely, and a fantastic place to walk. Inside is the breakfast room and living room, and set around the garden on the ground floor (Sue and Neill live upstairs) are the five lovely rooms. Barefoot, laid-back luxury.

Rooms: 5: 1 double, 1 queen, 2 twins, 1 king; all with en suite shower, 2 with baths as well.
Price: R375 – R575 pp sharing. Single supplement R150.
Meals: Full breakfast included. Kitchenette available for putting together salads and light meals.
Directions: From roundabout in Main St, go down hill past Central Beach, over Piesang River bridge. Over the circle, past shops (Kwikspar), right into Longships Ave. Straight over 3 speed bumps (2 km). Left into Gris Nez Dr. Over stop street, left into Gemini, 3rd street on L. Turn right and then left into Capricorn Lane.

Weldon Kaya

David and Gail Robinson
Cnr N2 and Piesang Valley Road, Plettenberg Bay, 6600
Tel: 044-533-2437 Fax: 044-533-4364
Email: info@weldonkaya.co.za Web: www.weldonkaya.com

Perched on the top of a hill, with views over Plettenberg Bay and the Robberg Peninsula, is the gloriously idiosyncratic Weldon Kaya, a riot of colour and imagination. David and Gail have created a haven for guests that is firmly afro-centric in its execution. All the ingredients of a successful guest house – comfort, friendly hosts, views etc – are there, but blended with a strong African sense of improvisation and rounded off with a lively open restaurant and bar. In the former you are seated in half an old tin bathtub on legs (with cushions!) at tables with old maps of Africa laminated into the surface, and illuminated by a chandelier of green bottles. David assisted the sculptor, his son, in the bottle-emptying phase – a noteworthy feat in itself. A ramp leads from the front door up to a lawn and plunge pool (a huge old water tank) on the very roof of the bar. Recycling is a strong theme across the whole property, including the cottages. All are different so take your pick from square, round, wooden, brick or clay and straw. Some have car windows built into the wall, some have more conventional apertures but you will sleep well in all of them. *Closed 3 weeks in June.*

Rooms: 10: 3 twins, 5 doubles, 2 family rooms, both with 1 double and 1 with bunk beds, the other with an extra bed. All have en/s bathrooms with shower.
Price: R250 – R400 pp sharing.
Meals: Full breakfast included. There is a restaurant as well: R80 – R90 per head.
Directions: On right as you come into Plett from George on the N2, before signpost to "Piesang Valley Road".

Bosavern

Vivienne Dreyer
38 Cutty Sark Ave, Plettenberg Bay, 6600
Tel: 044-533-1312 Fax: 044-533-0758
Email: info@bosavern.co.za Web: www.bosavern.co.za
Cell: 082-922-4721

The striking S-shaped waves of Bosavern's timbered ceiling mimic the sea and combine with minimalist white interiors and mirrors to strike a harmonious note with the blue ocean far below. Glass doors lead off the open-plan sitting room and onto the balcony where you can treat yourself on wicker chairs to a regal cliff-top view of the Robberg Peninsula and the white beaches of Plettenberg Bay. Powerful binoculars will pick out whales and schools of dolphins which are (can be!) plentiful in the clear water. The bedrooms downstairs have the same sliding doors that disappear smoothly into the wall and the sea breeze wafts in through a square gap of sky as if from a bright blue painting. The view from your room and private balcony is no less spectacular. Comfort is a priority, with goose-down duvets on enormous beds, fine cotton sheets, a welcoming bottle of Nederberg, gowns and slippers. Vivienne and Gerald are natural hosts, who provide great breakfasts and also picnic hampers for the beach or Robberg hikes, and mountain bikes and canoes for the madly active (a pool caters for loungers). They will also point you in the right direction for golf, and recommend a number of restaurants within easy walking distance.

Rooms: 5: 4 twins/doubles, 1 double; 3 with en/s shower; 2 with en/s bath and hand showers.
Price: R320 – R555 pp sharing. Single supplement 50% out of season, 80% in season.
Meals: Full breakfast included and served between 8 and 9 am. Other meals and occasional braais on request.
Directions: From Knysna take N2. Right at Shell garage into Plettenberg Bay. Turn 1st right into Cutty Sark Ave. Follow road round, then turn right again into cul-de-sac. House on left.

Beacon Lodge

Al and Clo Scheffer
57 Beacon Way, Plettenberg Bay, 6600
Tel: 044-533-2614
Fax: 044-533-2614
Email: beaconlodge@worldonline.co.za

This is a small (just two rooms) personal, friendly and involving B&B – and I mean B&B in the proper sense where you share the house with your hosts. (Both rooms have their own separate entrances, mind you, if you want to slip about more furtively.) The patio (for breakfasts, garden bird-watching or reading) has long views out to sea and it's only a short walk to the beach and the lagoon, presumably where you will want to spend at least some of your time. To this end Al and Clo have all beach necessities at the ready – umbrellas, towels and the like. The larger of the two rooms was my favourite (and also the more expensive – my wife will tell you this is typical) with sea views through a huge window and anti-glare solar blinds. There is seagrass on floors, plenty of immaculate seaside white in walls and towels and colour is added in the form of fresh flowers. The Scheffers take the greatest care of their guests. *Fridge facilities provided. Great restaurants within walking distance. Whales and dolphins in season. Closed Mid-Dec – mid-Jan and either June or July. Enquire first!*

Rooms: 2: 1 twin, 1 double, both with en/s bathrooms with showers.
Price: R165 – R330 pp sharing. Single rates on request.
Meals: Full breakfast included. There are good restaurants in town for other meals.
Directions: From Knysna take the N2. Take the second turn into Plett at the Engen garage – the house is 600 metres on your left.

Map Number 4

Aasvoelkrans

Jeanne Alston

1 van Riebeeck St, Montagu, 6720
Tel: 023-614-1228 Fax: 023-614-1228
Email: jeanne@aasvoelkrans.co.za Web: www.aasvoelkrans.co.za
Cell: 082-552-4545

Jeanne's enthusiasm for her guests and Montagu are in equal and ample measure. She was born and brought up here and her knowledge of the area is second to none. There are a multitude of good hikes in the surrounding hills, including the mountain behind the house (a handy one and a half hours up and down). Jeanne will fetch you from longer walks to avoid the tedium of returning the same way. The house itself and cottages had to be rebuilt a few years ago after a fire and were designed by Melanie, their daughter and award-winning architect. A rounded corrugated roof, wood pillars and beams, plain whites on walls and big plates of glass are warmed by bright splashes of colour, soft furniture and an African motif, which is tastefully woven in. Carved animals pop up unexpectedly, indoors and out, sometimes from large buckets of fresh flowers and Jeanne is rightly proud of her large, child-friendly garden. Each cottage has underfloor heating in winter and its own stoep to watch starry summer nights or enjoy the bright sunshine. Great style, even better hosting. *Only two hours from Cape Town. Enjoy the splendour of Arabian horses, African guinea-fowl and Rhodesian ridgeback dogs at Aasvoelkrans.*

Rooms: 3 cottages: 1 family (double and twin); 1 with double and 1 with twin; all with en suite showers.
Price: From R250 – R300 pp sharing. Single and children rates on request.
Meals: Full breakfast included and served when guests are ready. Excellent restaurants in town for other meals.
Directions: From Cape Town N1 to Worcester. At Worcester turn onto R60 which becomes the R62 at Ashton. R62 to Montagu. First R just before entering the village. First house on your L. B&B signs at either end of village.

Mimosa Lodge

Andreas and Yvette Küng
Church St, Montagu, 6720
Tel: 023-614-2351 Fax: 023-614-2418
Email: mimosa@lando.co.za Web: www.mimosa.co.za

My flabber is gasted by what Andreas and Yvette have achieved since they left Switzerland and moved into their two-storey Edwardian townhouse in the middle of beautiful mountain-marooned Montagu (just four years ago). It helps that I adore Art Deco as there's a lot of it about: chandeliers, wardrobes, cabinets, revolving bookcases, chairs re-upholstered in daring colours. The bedrooms do not resemble each other one bit. Some are in the house, others in the dazzling flower garden, with its herbs and vegetables, orchard and black marble swimming pool. Colours are used with imagination throughout, some bold, some demure, but all give a true sense of luxury and space. Each suite has a CD player and all the rooms have a host of little extras: decanter of Muscadel, books, magazines, fresh fruit, chilled water for example. An old shop counter has become the bar where guests congregate (and salivate) before dinner. Andreas is a chef and uses fresh ingredients from Yvette's lovingly tended garden (she herself has planted 200 species) and people travel miles to sample his international variations on a South African theme. I recommend Mimosa for a special treat. *Children by arrangement.*

Rooms: 12: 7 twins, 5 doubles all with en/s bathrooms; 3 with bath and separate shower, 5 with shower, 4 with baths/showers.
Price: R265 – R700 pp sharing. R390 – R1020 for singles.
Meals: Full breakfast included. Dinner (table d'hôte) in the restaurant R130.
Directions: Ask when booking, but Mimosa Lodge is clearly sign-posted in Montagu!

Merwenstein Fruit and Wine Farm

Hugo and Heidi van der Merwe

8 km from Bonnievale on Swellendam Road, PO Box 35, Bonnievale, 6730
Tel: 023-616-2806 Fax: 023-616-2806
Email: merwenstein@lando.co.za Web: www.merwenstein.co.za
Cell: 082-377-6638

'Merwenstein', in the Breede River Valley, derives from the merging of Hugo's and Heidi's surnames (she was previously a Steiner) and this spirit of happy co-operation thrives throughout the farm. The two of them take it in turns to guide guests on walks and show them the various fruit- and wine-related processes. The farm produces grapes for wine-making, but the emphasis is on fruit for fruit's sake, with apricots, plums galore, three varieties of peach and newly-planted persimmons. Hugo grew up on a neighbouring holding and has been farming at Merwenstein for over 20 years. Guests stay in an annexe with a gigantic (100 square metres, according to my iffy stride pattern) glass-fronted living room looking out over the farm. It's all tremendously light and airy and a great place for breakfast. Three comfortable bedrooms, combinations of pale walls and dark wall hangings, look into the garden, and for dinner you are encouraged to come up to the main farmhouse where you can learn more about Heidi's work with the local communities. Foremost among her projects is 'Lys Se Kombuis', where a former farm worker welcomes visitors to her home and her speciality 'vetkoek'. Delay that diet for a few more days.

Rooms: 3: all with en suite shower.
Price: R195 – R225 pp sharing. No single supplement as there is an extra single room available.
Meals: Full breakfast included. Dinners R75 – R95 including wine.
Directions: Use the same turn-off as for the Merwespont Wine Cellar, 8 km from Bonnievale on the road to Swellendam.

The Port-Wine Guest House

Chris and Andrea Nel
7 Queen St, Calitzdorp, 6660
Tel: 044-213-3131 Fax: 044-213-3131
Email: info@portwine.net Web: www.portwine.net

The key to the Port-Wine is Andrea herself who juggles a young family and her excellent guest house with kindness, energy and a sense of humour. No fingers wag and no tongues tut-tut. You can dress up for (excellent) dinners if you want, or you can shuffle up, like I did, in whatever rags you woke up in. Evening meals are a major feature at the Port-Wine (as Andrea is such a good cook, although *she* doesn't seem to think so) and everyone eats together, including husband Chris. The Nels have tried to remain faithful to the house's 1830s origins, saving what yellowwood they could from the ceilings and recycling it into dressers and beds; the new ceilings are of reed and beams. Four-poster beds are solid and firm with lacy canopies. During the day guests can lounge round the pool, visit the port wine growers, explore the spectacular mountain passes nearby; or in the evening climb the mountain and count the satellites when the sun goes down. Andrea, who is a registered tour guide, will also gladly take guests around their own ostrich and fruit farm. *The house is in the heart of Route 62 country.*

Rooms: 6: 3 doubles and 3 twins; 5 with en suite shower, 1 with shower and bath.
Price: R190 – R375 pp sharing. Single rates on request.
Meals: Full breakfast included and served from 8-10 a.m. 3-course dinners R85 – R95.
Directions: Calitzdorp is on the R62 between Ladismith and Oudtshoorn. Ask for precise directions when booking or follow the road signs.

The Retreat at Groenfontein

Marie and Grant Burton

PO Box 240, Calitzdorp, 6660
Tel: 044-213-3880 Fax: 044-213-3880
Email: groenfon@iafrica.com Web: http://users.iafrica.com/g/gr/groenfon/

A tiny gravel road twists along the sides of this idyllic valley, beside the river that gives the Retreat its name, while abandoned Cape Dutch farm buildings line the route which eventually leads to the Burtons' Victorian-colonial homestead. They ran a popular wilderness lodge in Namibia before trawling southern Africa for a new Eden, and it took years to find Groenfontein. It was worth the wait. The view from the verandah – where guests eat once they've been persuaded to sit down – crosses a valley and climbs the Burtons' own mountain before joining the vast Swartberg Nature Reserve. What with the hiking trails that Grant and Marie are cutting, the opportunities for merry traipsing are limitless. If (when!) it gets hot, you can swim in river or pool, or collapse inside the gloriously cool house. Many original furnishings remain, including marble fireplaces and pine and yellowwood flooring, while much of the newer stuff has been built by Grant himself. "He's very handy," says Marie admiringly. Airy bedrooms benefit from simple combinations of blues, whites and pale woods, with duvet and curtain designs of Marie's own creation. This is an incredible area to explore – kloofs, mountain wilderness, half-forgotten roads etc – but you can always come home to hearty meals, welcoming hosts and a truly relaxed household. You will want at least two nights.

Rooms: 5: 2 doubles and 3 twins; 2 with en suite bath; 3 with en suite shower.
Price: R290 – R390 pp sharing. Single rates on request.
Meals: Breakfast and 3-course dinners included.
Directions: From Oudtshoorn take R62 towards Calitzdorp for 30 km. Turn R onto dirt road signed Kruisrivier. After 17 km keep L at fork as road gets narrower and follow for 10.7 km until see sign for Burton's to your R. From Calitzdorp L at Groenfontein sign – 19 km to house. Drive slowly on these roads.

Klein Karoo, Western Cape

Bisibee

Isabé Fourie

171 Church St, Oudtshoorn, 6625
Tel: 044-272-4784 Fax: 044-279-2373
Email: bisibee@hotmail.com Cell: 082-460-7556
Web: www.centralres.co.za/southafrica/westcape/oudtshoorn/bisibee/bisibee.html

With a name like Bisibee you wouldn't expect a super-slick interior designer's playground, all black and chrome and minimalist furnishing. And sure enough you don't get it. Isabé is probably the sweetest lady in Oudtshoorn (and if she isn't I would like introductions effected immediately). Her colonial-style house is framed by a very green garden full of bougainvillea, palms (for shade) and suffused with flowers, while a trampoline stretched at ground level and a small swimming pool will keep children running from one to the other. There are tall pot plants, white pillars and green awnings on the verandah where adults take tea at a more sedate pace. Inside, the bedrooms are large with brass beds, wood floors, unfettered wall colours (one room is pink), plenty of frill in the furnishings and an honesty fridge. Isabé provides tea for her guests on arrival, and from that moment on could not look after you with more warmth or greater application. People file glowing reports in her vistor's book because *they* insist, not her. *Oudtshoorn is the capital town of the Klein Karoo – much magnificent mountain scenery and a lot of talk about ostriches.*

Rooms: 4: 2 doubles and 2 twins, 2 with en/s bath, 2 with en/s showers.
Price: From R180 – R220 pp sharing. Singles from R220 – R240.
Meals: Full breakfast included. Dinner available on request R75 (3 courses).
Directions: Coming into Oudtshooorn from George, turn left at 3rd traffic lights. Go over one crossroads and Bisibee is on the left.

Map Number 3

Onse Rus

Lisa and Gary Smith
47 Church St, Prince Albert, 6930
Tel: 023-541-1380 Fax: 023-541-1064
Email: lisass@intekom.co.za
Cell: 083-629-9196

The official pamphlet does a good job of conveying the delights of Onse Rus, but it modestly fails to bear testament to the biggest plus, the Smiths themselves. 'Talking shop' was never meant to be this much fun. They fell in love with Prince Albert and the 150-year-old Cape Dutch Onse Rus in 1999 and their enthusiasm for both town and house has not abated since. Guests who have come down over the Swartberg Pass are given a whisky for their nerves, those who haven't can go up there with Gary. He'll even take you to The Hell, a famously isolated community 57 km down a dirt track. Back at the house, the large living room is hung with a permanent exhibition of local artists' work. The four thatched bedrooms all have private entrances, high ceilings, white walls and simple Karoo furnishings. One used to be part of the bakery, another was the printing room for a local newspaper. The house has some history! Lunch is available from Wednesday to Sunday, and if the weather permits – it usually does – you can sit out on the verandah and enjoy fig ice cream in the shade of the Cape Ash and Karoo Pepper trees

Rooms: 4: 2 doubles and 2 twins (one twin sleeps 4). All with en suite shower.
Price: R180 – R215 pp sharing. Single prices enthusiastically given on request.
Meals: Pub lunches Wednesdays – Sundays. Dinner on request if restaurants fully booked.
Directions: On the main street (Kerk or Church St) on corner of Church and Bank Sts.

Dennehof Karoo Guest Houses

Neill and Elaine Hurford
Prince Albert, 6930
Tel: 023-541-1227 Fax: 023-541-1158
Email: hurford@gem.co.za Web: http://home.intekom.com/dennehof/
Cell: 082-412-6505

Numerous guesthouses in this region offer a "genuine Karoo experience", but few can make the claim quite as truthfully as Dennehof. The 1835 building and its outhouses, which back onto the desert on the edge of Prince Albert, have been completely restored by the Hurfords and the results are a joy to see. The whitewashed buildings still have many of their original clay-and-straw walls, ceilings are made of poplar and reeds, and bathrooms are in keeping with the vernacular. Much of the 'new' furniture, such as yellowwood doors and ancient stoves, has been sourced from old Karoo homes. And where modern methods were unavoidable, they were used sympathetically. For example, a facsimile was made of the dairy's crumbling clay floor so that it could be recast in cement. Guests stay in what were the dairy, wagon shed and cow shed, or self-cater in the farm-workers' cottage, now called The Olive House. Although you are accommodated "within the parameters of the desert" says Neill, warmed by stoves in winter and naturally cooled in summer, there are discreet additional comforts such as wall panel heaters and electric blankets. Lastly and importantly, the Hurfords are fascinating hosts, and Elaine has eight books about South Africa to her name. They are both hugely enthusiastic about the Karoo and guests invariably leave with similar passions. *There is a little reservoir for dips in summer.*

Rooms: 4: 2 doubles, 1 twin, 1 cottage (double and twin). 3 with en suite showers and 2 baths in the cottage.
Price: R195 – R225 pp sharing B&B in the Wagon Shed. No single supplement. R150 – R175 pp self-catering in the Olive House.
Meals: Full breakfast included. Dinners by special arrangement for parties of more than five.
Directions: From the N1, go through Prince Albert to the end and Dennehof is on the left. From Meiringspoort or Swartberg, Dennehof is on the right before you enter the town.

Collins House

Tessa and Sheila Collins

63 Kerk St (Church St), Prince Albert, 6930
Tel: 023-541-1786 Fax: 023-541-1786
Cell: 082-377-1340

Collins House stands out on Kerkstraat, unusual as a two-storey Victorian townhouse among so many Cape Dutch gable buildings. The open-plan kitchen/sitting room is the warm heart of the house – check out the beautiful tile and wood floor – and Tessa's office is an old desk in the middle of the room. There are doors out to the flower garden, and the very large swimming pool and air-con in all the bedrooms are a blessing during Karoo summers. The town is full of Cape Dutch national monuments and snoozes right at the foot of the spectacular Swartberg pass. You must not fail to experience this and Tessa takes guests up there with evening drinks – or you can hire your own scooter in town. Collins House is long on luxury. Bedrooms are upstairs (almost a rarity in itself in South Africa) and you are mollied and coddled with fine-quality linens and lotions. Luxury is one thing, but character is inimitable... and Tessa, Sheila and Collins House have that in spades. *No children. DSTV is available in the upstairs bedroom.*

Rooms: 3: all twins; 1 with en suite bath, 1 with shower and 1 with bath and shower.
Price: R170 – R350 pp sharing. Single supplement R70.
Meals: Full breakfast included and served till 9.30 a.m.
Directions: On Kerkstraat in the middle of town.

56 Kerkstraat B&B

Herman and Susan Perold
Prince Albert, 6930
Tel: 023-541-1768 Fax: 023-541-1768
Email: perold@netactive.co.za

The only contrivance of this sweet 1841 Cape Dutch gable house is a new en suite bathroom tacked sympathetically onto the back. The high reed ceilings in the 'voorkamer' (front room) are 160 years old and all the renovations used as much of the original structure as was safe. The results are intimate and homely – thatched roof, wood floors, thick round beams. The house seems to gravitate towards the wide stoep at the back with its distant views of the Swartberg Mountains. The garden even contains a young vineyard, the first crop maturing in experimental vats in Paarl – 2003 should see the first proper harvest. The two guest rooms are downstairs while the Perolds climb a spiral staircase to an open-plan loft. The style is country simple, solid and of good quality – beds firm, shower powerful, mosquito nets effective. A word of warning – do not eat too much for dinner the night before. Breakfast chez Perold is substantial. You eat on the stoep (many of the dishes are pottered by friends) and probably to Mozart. Everything is home-made or locally grown – free-range eggs, croissants, and breads and jams, local cheeses, apricots, olives. The Perolds, who hail from Stellenbosch (Herman had several years at Oxford, too), clearly enjoy the extra perspective their guests bring with them. Herman is a chemist/microbiologist/philosopher so steer the conversation in that direction at your peril!

Rooms: 2: 1 double with en suite shower; 1 twin with private shower and bath.
Price: R150 – R200 pp sharing.
Meals: Full breakfast included and flexible about times.
Directions: From Oudtshoorn either over Swartberg Pass or through Meiringspoort into Prince Albert. Left into Kerk St – house past the church opposite hotel. From N1, turn off at Prince Albert Road (railway siding), 45 km south leads directly into Kerk St, house on left side.

Lemoenfontein Game Lodge

Ingrid Köster

Beaufort West, 6970
Tel: 023-415-2847 Fax: 023-415-1044
Email: lemoen@mweb.co.za Web: www.lemoenfontein.co.za

Lemoenfontein, in the shadow of the Nuweveld Mountains, is one of those places where whatever your mood on arrival – and after a tiring drive down the N1 mine was ropey – a calmness envelops you like magic vapour. I was suddenly enjoying a cool drink on the vast wooden verandah, gazing over measureless miles of veld, and chatting happily to Ingrid about the history of the place. It was built as a hunting lodge in 1850, then became a sanatorium for TB sufferers (the dry Karoo air was beneficial), a farm and finally (and still) a nature reserve. Everything has been done well here, no corners cut and the result is a most relaxing, hassle-free stay. Rooms are stylish and understated with top quality fabrics and completely comfortable beds. Outside, lawns, a new cactus garden and the veld are all segregated by high drystone walls. You *must* go on a game drive through the reserve before dinner – to look at all the buck and zebra of course, but also to be out in such scenery as the sun goes down. And one final thing: dinner when we got back was at first mouth-watering, then lip-smacking. A real South African experience.

Rooms: 13: 6 twins, 7 doubles. All with en/s bathrooms, 7 with baths and 6 with showers.
Price: R260 – R280 pp sharing. R50 single supplement.
Meals: Full breakfast included. A set dinner is available every night.
Directions: From the N1, 2 km north of Beaufort West. Go left at the sign to Lemoenfontein. Go 4 km up dirt track, following signs.

Northern Cape

Papkuilsfontein Farmhouse

Willem and Mariëtte van Wyk, Jaco and Alrie
Nieuwoudtville, 8180
Tel: 027-218-1246 Fax: 027-218-1246
Email: reservations@papkuilsfontein.com
Web: www.papkuilsfontein.com

I'm going to stick my neck out and say that this is my favourite place to stay in South Africa! And here are my reasons. You stay in an old stone cottage, surrounded by rock, gum tree and wildlife, not another human in sight. The quality of peace and stillness defeats description. Gas-fired plumbing for baths, hurricane lamps for light – many guests have refused to come back if Willem installs electricity. Then there's the small matter of the gorge and waterfall, which I would have kept secret if I wasn't insistent on your visiting the farm. Your jaw will drop 200 metres into the canyon. Take a picnic to the deep rock pools for swimming above the waterfall and you can climb down into the gorge in an hour and a half. The wild flowers in season are sensational even by Namaqualand standards; the plantlife, divided between Cape fynbos and Karoo succulent, a botanist's dream; steenbok, klipspringer, porcupine and dassie love the terrain and have NOT been specially introduced; Mariëtte is an excellent cook (breakfast a string of surprises). It's a magical place that not many know about and the van Wyks are lovely, friendly people who seem unable to put a proper price on what they have to offer! You should stay *at least* two nights.

Rooms: 2 stone cottages sleeping 4 and 6; one has bath, one has shower.
Price: R205 – R255 pp sharing. Single rates +R50.
Meals: Full breakfast included. 3-course dinners R85.
Directions: From CT take N1 then N7 to Vanrhynsdorp. Turn off onto R27 to Nieuwoudtville. R into town, and straight thro' onto dirt road for 22 km. Farm signed to R.

Naries Guest Farm

Allan du Preez
Route R355, Springbok/Kleinzee, Springbok, 8240
Tel: 027-712-2462 Fax: 027-712-2462

It's a long and dusty drive to this remote corner of South Africa, but as always with remote corners, it's well worth the effort. Big barren hills march off in a vast and dramatic landscape to the sea 120 km away at Port Nolloth. Whatever you think of the flamboyant, seventies-inspired décor at Naries I guarantee you will love the place before leaving! Allan puts so much effort into your welcome and stay that there is often moisture in the eye on departure. By day you can read by the new swimming pool, go hiking, or visit the Richtersveld National Park. In spring the Namaqualand wild flower extravaganza is one of the wonders of the world, although you will need to book very early. Guests are taken up to a hillside lapa for an almost surreal glass of sherry at sunset. The view to the sea from the 700-metre Southern African Escarpment is spectacular and you might see duiker, springbok or baboons on the way. And finally the candlelit meal on your return is a triumph – I can still recall Allan's malva pudding at will. The greatest possible care is taken at Naries and friends are made here. Try and arrive in the early afternoon. They have added a small pool to cool off in since the last edition.

Rooms: 4: 3 doubles and 1 twin; 3 with en/s shower, 1 with en/s bath.
Price: R325 – R425 pp sharing for dinner B&B. Single R355 – R455 for dinner B&B. Also a simple cottage sleeping 5 at R400 a night.
Meals: Dinner and a full breakfast included in the price. Cottage self-catering.
Directions: In Springbok take van der Stel road west of Springbok – becomes the Kleinzee Road. Follow the dirt road for 27 km – the farm is signed on your right before you go down the mountain.

Bedrock

Grazia de Beer and Rose Cross
2 Beach Road, Port Nolloth, 8280
Tel: 027-851-8865 Fax: 027-851-8865
Email: bedrock@icon.co.za

I urge you to make the trip over the mountains to a unique and infrequently visited corner of the country for a taste of an African version of the Wild West. After a hundred or so kilometres of arid mountain you finally descend to those familiar smells of the sea… and there's usually a nip in the air too. Bring a jumper even if it is 40 degrees plus in Springbok. Bedrock is down on the sea front, a 130–year-old tongue-and-groove house imported from Denmark (yes, even in the 1870s the Scandinavians were experts in assemble-yourself pre-fab): guest house, junk store, museum, art gallery… and repository for scandalous Port Nolloth stories, which are not in short supply. The weatherboard walls reminded me of being on board ship and the house rambles and creaks with age, a thousand doors opening on each other, walls crowded with nautical paintings and unusual artefacts collected by owner-magpie, Grazia de Beer. Or you can stay in one of five other equally antique and charming cottages, with wonky windows, yellowwood floors and most have sea views. There's a tea garden where you can play chess and a swimming pool is constantly under discussion. You can swim, meanwhile, at the hotel, if you have lunch. Port Nolloth is supported by the diamond-diving industry and has an intriguingly ripe reputation as a frontier town. Grazia and Bedrock are a great bonus.

Rooms: 7: 5 cottages and 2 rooms in the house. The cottages mostly have 2 bedrooms, a sitting room, kitchen and a bathroom (let out to one party at a time).
Price: R100 – R200 pp sharing.
Meals: Breakfasts can be provided in fridge by request for R25.
Directions: From Springbok north on N7 to Steinkopf. Left onto the R382 to Port Nolloth where you drive straight to the sea and then turn right – Bedrock is just there on your right.

Eastern Cape

The Armagh Guest House

Johan and Marion Brink

24 Fynbos Ave, Storms River, Tsitsikamma, 6308
Tel: 042-281-1512 Fax: 042-281-1510
Email: stay@thearmagh.com   Web: www.thearmagh.com

Johan and Marion have added a zesty restaurant to the Armagh's zesty repertoire since we visited for the last edition. Rafters serves Cape-Malay food for up to twenty people, but, despite the extra work load this naturally brings, they are still taking life with a pinch of salt. This remains a fiercely unpretentious guest house, where the milk of human kindness prevails. The exterior of the building is red face-brick, while the rest is made almost entirely of pine with rolls of silver insulation lining the roof and adding to the feeling of space – the whole place is soundly eco-friendly. The main part of the building combines the restaurant, connected to the bar, and a little loft sitting area up wooden steps, which looks down over the scene – perfect for relaxing and observing life in the guest house. Outside, a conical mountain, Storms River Peak in the Tsitsikamma range, looms over the wild-tending indigenous garden, patched with small flower-bordered lawns. All the bedrooms open out onto this view and have vine-covered patios whence to enjoy it. Painted walls, snoring peacefully in low-key colours, are rudely awoken by dandy-bright cushions, counterpanes and abstract pictures. *The beach is minutes away, as is the world-famous Tsitsikamma National Park.*

Rooms: 5: 3 doubles, 2 twins all with en/s bathrooms, 3 baths, 2 showers.
Price: From R225 – R375 pp sharing. Single supplement 40%. We advise you to book in advance.
Meals: Full breakfast included. Meals available in Rafters Restaurant, 5 courses from R105.
Directions: 165 km from Port Elizabeth and 65 km from Plettenberg Bay. Turn off the N2 Highway into Storms River Village and you'll see The Armagh on the right.

34 Lovemore Crescent

Monica Johnson

PO Box 85, St Francis Bay, 6312
Tel: 042-294-0825 Fax: 042-294-0825
Email: dolfinvu@intekom.co.za Web: www.b-b.co.za
Cell: 082-695-3395

34 Lovemore is an unpretentious B&B, and an absolute delight. This has everything to do with Monica's warm hospitality and the character of her home, built 20 years ago, though the beachside location is an added bonus. Tea, scones and home-made biscuits appear on arrival, and you are then shown up to your quarters, two large rooms under a high thatched roof, with a living area between them, all looking out to sea. The small front garden has weaver-birds' nests in the trees and possibly Africa's most southerly baobab tree, a tenacious little thing brought down from Zimbabwe by the family in the '80s. And on the other side of the garden there is another separate flat, which can be rented on a B&B basis or as a self-catering unit (but you'd be missing out on a great breakfast…). It lacks the sea views, so Monica feels duty-bound to offer it at give-away prices. With a sweeping vista across St Francis Bay, where southern right whales can be seen in season and dolphins year-round, you cannot fail to relax here. Keen surfers will be interested to note (they will in fact salivate over the news) that Bruce's Beauties are at the end of the garden. *Closed mid-December to mid-January.*

Rooms: 2 rooms in the house; 1 double with en/s shower and 1 twin with private shower and bath. 1 flat sleeping up to 6 with 1 bathroom.
Price: Rooms in the house: R225 – R300 pp sharing. Flat: R125 pp self-catering, R150 pp with breakfast.
Meals: Full breakfast included for B&B in the house. Flat, as above.
Directions: From the Humansdorp road take 1st right into Lyme Rd South, then 3rd right onto St. Francis Drive, then 5th left onto Lovemore Crescent. 34 Lovemore is sign-posted at each of these turns. 34 is the last house on the left.

Map Number 4

Duxbury

Sheila Beckett
8 George Rd, St Francis Bay, 6312
Tel: 042-294-0514 Fax: 042-294-0514
Email: duxburybb@worldonline.co.za

Duxbury makes no claims to being anything more than a very friendly, dyed-in-the-wool B&B. You stay in Sheila's comfortable white-walled, thatched cottage in this quaint seaside village where strict planning regulations have ensured that almost all the other houses are thatched and white-walled too. Meet Sheila. She has an impish sense of humour and you are soon settled in, sipping a cup of tea, a conspirator in her tales of local, national and international matters. The guest rooms have private entrances and there is also a cottage in the garden. The white walls of the interior contrast with bright curtains and counterpanes and this lends the house a fresh and enlivening feel. A leisurely breakfast, made to order by Sheila, is quite a spread. The best B&Bs are places where both owner and guest get as much out of the experience as each other. I give you Duxbury. *Sheila will sort out Kromme River and Marina Canals cruises and golf. The house is just 100 metres from the sea for safe beach bathing.*

Rooms: 3: 1 twin and 2 doubles. 2 en/s bathrooms, 1 with bath and 1 with shower. 1 separate bathroom with shower.
Price: From R140 to R180 pp sharing or for singles.
Meals: Full breakfast included.
Directions: Take Humansdorp off-ramp on N2 freeway from Cape Town 80 km short of Port Elizabeth. Proceed down Humansdorp Main Street to T-junction opposite caravan park. Turn L to St. Francis Bay (18 km). Take first turning L, 2 km after crossing Kromme River Bridge and follow signs to Duxbury.

Fairfield

Bev Campbell

Willowtree Farm, Addo, 6105
Tel: 042-233-0379
Email:
bevcampbell@intekom.co.za

Fairfield is a simple, comfortable and extremely friendly bed and breakfast, rather than a guest house. It is very much Bev's home, shared with her guests so openly and generously that you will feel at home yourself before too many minutes have elapsed. And you will certainly be adopted by the omnipresent Jack Russells… don't think they have reserved their affections for just you! The house is on the Sundays River, surrounded by a well-tended garden and orchards lie beyond. It sits plum in the middle of Willowtree Farm, a working citrus farm (no plums), close to Addo town and the elephant park itself. A perfect base from which to go and marvel at these giant creatures, particularly if you are on a budget. The park is one of the best places to see elephants in the country and the entrance fee stood at R15 when I visited! Bev will point you in the right direction for any number of things to do in the area. If you don't fancy going anywhere, however, I recommend a walk through the citrus groves, or you can just sit and look at them from the vantage point of the large stoep and chat to Bev.

Rooms: 2: 1 with en/s shower and bath, 1 with shared bathroom with shower and bath, 1 single.
Price: R150 – R175 pp sharing. Single price is the same.
Meals: Full breakfast included.
Directions: Ask for directions when you book.

Woodall Farm

James and Debbie Miller
Jan Smuts Ave, Addo, 6105
Tel: 042-233-0128 Fax: 042-233-0128
Email: miller@woodall-addo.co.za Web: www.woodall-addo.co.za

I arrived at Woodall Farm in the middle of a heat wave, but I still found a cool spot under the thatch, overlooking the dam. I sat and wrote mango-juice-fuelled notes, while an Egyptian goose, her goslings and Debbie's two pet swans pottered around me – very relaxing. James and Debbie run a lovely, tranquil guest house in the Miller family home. As you might expect, there is plenty of family history on the walls and in the fabric of the place. The picture in the sitting room of James' grandfather's first house gives away the family's distant origins, a croft in the Orkneys. Woodall is an ideal place from which to visit Addo Elephant Park and I'm sure many arrive with this in mind. But the farm has so many charms of its own that many guests will stay 'at home' to make full use of the swimming pool, rose-filled garden and bar and the deck overlooking the dam. The onus is on taking it easy, and it is difficult not to. Huge, pine-floored bedrooms have wall-to-wall windows, a private patio surrounded by bougainvillea and a view over the orchards. Five also have outside showers, great for cooling off before wonderful dinners, which is served overlooking the water – Debbie is an accomplished chef.

Rooms: 7: 4 doubles, 3 twins all with baths and showers en/s. 5 of them have outside showers.
Price: R450 – R750 pp sharing. 50% supplement for single occupancy.
Meals: Full breakfast included and served to 9am. Light lunches available. 3 course gourmet dinners also available – from R95.
Directions: 4.5 km past Addo on the R335, turn left and Woodall Farm is sign-posted 1.5 km after that.

River Bend Country Lodge

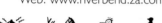

Jennifer Gird
Addo
Tel: 042-233-0161 Fax: 042-233-0162
Email: reservations@riverbend.za.com
Web: www.riverbend.za.com

At River Bend, expect the apogee of luxury in all things. This is a matter of pride. Private cottages, huge beds, state-of-the-art bathrooms, pristine swimming pool (the sort that you can swim up and down in), immaculate and ripening garden (a mix of English rose garden and indigenous veld plants); and attentive, friendly staff who don't overdo it and allow you properly to relax. There are a plethora of cool spaces to hide in, a library, a bar, your own cottage patio. And meals are all superb, breakfast a moveable feast, dinner a highlight, served in an elegant (but not intimidating) dining room. So much space and privacy for so few rooms. I ticked off the bedroom extras without surprise: aircon, D(igital)S(attelite)TV, toiletries in large bottles, gowns and slippers in cupboards, laundry returned wrapped in tissue paper, imported linen. You have basically whatever you want. But all this pampering takes place in the middle of untamed bush. Your bedroom doors open onto wild veld and now the River Bend reserve has been swallowed up by the greater good of the Addo Elephant Park, with elephants to be introduced to River Bend this year. All these extraordinary bonuses are underpinned by a genuinely friendly, truly relaxed, highly luxurious country lodge experience… rather than the rough and tumble of a game lodge. *Giraffe, gemsbok, zebra, eland, sable and waterbuck already roam the reserve.*

Rooms: 8 suites: all twins/kings with en suite bath and shower.
Price: R1170 – R1800 pp sharing. Singles R1550 – R2000. Children 12 and under R730, free for under threes. Winter specials.
Meals: Full breakfast included. Dinner: R180.
Directions: From Addo follow straight on R335 for 11.5 km. Turn left signed Zuurberg. After 3.5 km River Bend gates are on your right.

Cosmos Cuisine

Elzona Deetlefs

Main Street, Sunland,
Addo, 6115
Tel: 042-234-0323
Fax: 042-234-0323
Email:
info@cosmoscuisine.co.za
Web:
www.cosmoscuisine.co.za

As my predecessor in this oft-envied job found, Cosmos Cuisine lives up to its name. The food here is out of this world! While Sam fell for the puddings, particularly the chocolate ones, I was enraptured by the springbok carpaccio, though the apple cake was something else too. The restaurant is informal, but smart (or vice versa, you decide), with wrought-iron tables and chairs, and people come from far and wide for lunch and dinner. Lucky you – to sample Elzona's cooking it's only a short stroll across the wide lawn from your room. The emphasis at Cosmos is on relaxation, and the accommodation certainly reflects that. The bedrooms are full of open spaces with big beds and white linen. The flower-edged garden and terrace outside the main building offer cool shady spots, and a rock pool, useful in summer if you're hot after a visit to the Elephant Park. Finally, Elzona's obvious warmth and kindness set the temperature at Cosmos. *Riding available on nearby farms.*

Rooms: 10 rooms; 2 family rooms, 1 double, 7 twins. All with en/s bathrooms; 1 with shower, 3 with baths, 6 with both.
Price: R350 – R500 pp sharing. +50% for singles.
Meals: Full breakfast included. Dinner available in the restaurant.
Directions: R335 from Port Elizabeth through Addo – over the railway line. First left (sign to Kirkwood R336) – 8 km into Sunland you'll see the sign to Cosmos Cuisine on your left.

The Elephant House

Clive and Anne Read
PO Box 82, Addo, 6105
Tel: 042-233-2462 Fax: 042-233-0393
Email: elephanthouse@intekom.co.za
Web: www.elephanthouse.co.za   Cell: 083-799-5671

The bush telegraph gave advance notice of the many charms at Elephant House. Many tourists and other guest house owners had urged us to visit with a sincerity you could not ignore. It's a stunning house, the brainchild of one night's sleepless pondering by Anne who mapped the whole thing out in her head – a small lawned courtyard surrounded on three sides by thatched and shady verandah. The house is in a sense inside out. The drawing room leads to a dining room outside on the verandah (with antiques and Persian rugs). All the bedrooms open onto the verandah too and dinner (advertised with an African gong) is served there on silver and crystal. Evening meals are lit with lampshades made of Tuareg bowls to stunning effect. Lawns, indigenous trees and the racehorse stud (Clive used to run one in Natal too) surround the house and when I was there the paddocks were full of mares with their foals. The bedrooms are luxurious with antique furniture, carpets, thick duvets and deep beds; and morning tea or coffee is brought to your bed, if so desired. *Only minutes from Addo Elephant Park.*

Rooms: 8: 4 twins, 4 doubles, all with en/s bathrooms all with shower and bath. 2 have outdoor showers.
Price: R400 – R700 (low season), R600 – R1000 (high season) pp sharing. Single supplement + 50%.
Meals: Full breakfast included. Lunch and dinner available by arrangement. Dinners – 3 courses from R110.
Directions: From P.E. R335 through Addo 5 km on the road towards the park – you will see a sign off to your left for The Elephant House.

Map Number 5

Proctorsfontein Farmhouse and Hermitage

Brian Rippon
P.O. Box 400, Nr. Grahamstown, 6140
Tel: 046-622-2382 Fax: 046-622-2382
Email: rippon@imaginet.co.za

Brian Rippon is the perfect host and gentleman (he won't like me saying!): attentive, well-travelled, amusing company and unreasonably humble about all that he, a tri-lingual artist and vet, and Proctorsfontein, his well-loved and lived-in 150-year-old homestead, have to offer. That's why he needs me to blow his trumpet for him… which I think I've just done! You stay as house guests with breakfast, dinner, any drives in the country or out on the cattle farm (when they happen), even drinks (within reason) included in the price. So dump your bags, go for a swim in the pool, take a turn in the garden (the farm has long views over the Assegai River Valley) and join Brian when you're ready for drinks and dinner. Solid country cooking is based on roasts and the like, prepared by housekeeper Poppy, and Brian has many fine wines. Or a braai can be arranged at the family's tented camp in the wilderness. The bedrooms have delightfully faded edges, books everywhere, Brian's accomplished landscapes on the walls and pots of impatience (the flower not the mood) to brighten the day. Hearty farmhouse breakfasts are served on the black slate patio. This is a place where I felt instantly at home. *Dam fishing available. Proctorsfontein is half an hour from Shamwari and Kariega Game Reserve; 1 hour from Addo Elephant Park.*

Rooms: 2: 1 double room with private bathroom. 1 upstairs apartment with twin room and en/s shower.
Price: R350 – 450 pp sharing.
Meals: Full breakfast and dinner included.
Directions: From Port Elizabeth 80 km on the National Road to Grahamstown (N2). Turn off to Sidbury on gravel road for 20 km to Proctorsfontein.

Leeuwenbosch Country House

Bill & Rosemary Fowlds

Paterson, 6130
Tel: 042-235-1252 Fax: 042-235-1252
Email: fowldsg@iafrica.com Web: www.amakhala.com
Cell: 082-460-8902 or 083-627-9285

Leeuwenbosch has gone from strength to strength since our first edition and remains one of the best finds in South Africa. Although now firmly established as the senior partner in the Amakhala Game Reserve, it has lost none of its zest or character, while gradually building its portfolio. Bill' tiny cellar pub remains an intimate forum for story-telling for example. There's a whole lot more game in the reserve now… more wildebeest, impala, zebra, giraffe, gemsbok, eland and some 'big five' are being introduced this year. A new lodge with four luxury rooms has also been added just up from the Victorian guest house with its beautiful antique snooker table and portraits of only marginally less beautiful antique Fowlds. Dinners, served either at a bush camp after a game drive or back in the dining room above the pub, remain intimate, convivial and delicious, thanks to Rosemary. And finally there is Eliweni, a simple, secluded wooden lodge, its deck jutting proudly forth from a high cliff-top. The views out over the flood plain and the reserve's fifteen kilometres of Bushman's River are stunning!

Rooms: 9 : 4 rooms in the guest house, 3 twins, 1 dbl, 3 en/s bathrooms, 1 private. 4 double rooms in lodge all with en/s shower & bath, 1 wooden lodge (sleeps 5).
Price: From R650 – 1195 pp sharing fully inclusive of meals, game drives. Singles on request. Call for off-season rates.
Meals: Full breakfast included and served until 9.30 am. Dinners also included in the price.
Directions: From P.E. take the N2 to Grahamstown (do not take Paterson) for 67 km where you'll see signs for Leeuwen Bosch on your right only 1.5 km after Shamwari turn on the left.

Settlers Hill Cottages

Marthie Hendry
71 Hill Street, Grahamstown, 6140
Tel: 046-622-9720 Fax: 046-622-9720
Email: hadeda@imaginet.co.za
Web: www.imaginet.co.za/settlershillcottages   Cell: 082-809-3395

Marthie Hendry's passion for Grahamstown and its history is infectious and will envelop you if you stay in one of her delightful cottages, built and originally inhabited by British settlers in the 1820s. The three smallest are national monuments near the evocatively-named Artificers Square, the city's original artisan quarter: Sheblon, an intimate, thatched cottage; Custard Apple Cottage, which you may have to share with the benign ghost of Grandpa West; and the Coach House, previously a carpentry workshop, Grandma West's sweet shop and, presumably, a coach house. Jasmine, with its separate garden cottage, and Bellhambra Cottages are larger, but similar in charm and character. The decoration throughout is a blend of original features (such as Oregon pine floors) and modern where it matters (i.e. in bathrooms and kitchens), but the notable lack of ostentation only adds to the authenticity. You will be hard-pushed to take any of it in, however, if you attempt everything on Marthie's Things-to-Do-in-Grahamstown list, which is as long as a man's arm. She is on the tourism board for the city and loves taking people around the imposing Victorian buildings in town or to the witch-doctor shop nearby, where a Xhosa herbalist can mix you up some good luck potions.

Rooms: 5 cottages from 1 bed to 3 beds. 1 cottage where Marthie does B&B: 3 bedrooms all with en/s bathrooms.
Price: From R145 pp self-catering. B&B from R180 pp sharing. Single supplement varies according to how long you're staying.
Meals: Full breakfast can be included. (See above.) There are a number of restaurants within walking distance.
Directions: Marthie meets guests at 71 Hill St., which intersects the High Street at the Cathedral. No. 71 is 3 blocks up the hill or ask for directions when booking.

The Cock House

Peter and Belinda Tudge

10 Market St, Grahamstown, 6140
Tel: 046-636-1287 Fax: 046-636-1287
Email: cockhouse@imaginet.co.za Web: www.cockhouse.co.za
Cell: 082-820-5592

The Cock House celebrated its 10th anniversary as a guest house last June, which puts it firmly in the veteran category in South African terms, and its longevity is easy to understand. Like me, Messrs Mandela and Mbeki enjoy staying here (unlike me, their visits are commemorated in photos on the walls of the bar). The Tudges are fun and great to chat to, and their staff genuinely happy to be working here, which is most of the battle won. The house is old (1826) and rooms are named after previous owners, most recently South African author André Brink. A stone floored verandah stretches along the front of the house (mirrored by a wooden balcony upstairs) and the interior is full of native yellowwood in floors, ceilings and bar. The pub is also for locals an opportunity to strike up a conversation, and is usually hosted by Peter – I think this is his favourite part of the job. I can also recommend the restaurant, which has its own herb garden and uses local and seasonal ingredients wherever possible. The two large rooms in the main house have glass doors opening onto the balcony and the four converted stables open onto the garden. Personal and fun. Belinda is also a guide accredited to take tours round historic Grahamstown.

Rooms: 7: 2 twins, 5 doubles all with en/s bathroom with bath and shower, 1 with shower, 1 with bath. A self-catering flat with 2 twin rooms.
Price: R250 – R300 pp sharing. R300 – R350 for singles.
Meals: Full breakfast included and served until anytime. Lunch and dinner available in the restaurant (except Sunday lunch). Dinners from R95.
Directions: From P.E. take 2nd exit from N2 signposted "Business District/George Street". Take off-ramp L, turn at bridge into George St. Continue down long hill into Grahamstown. At 4-way stop with Market St turn R and you will see the Cock House on the right corner.

The Loerie Hide

Sue and Nigel Rainer
2B Sheerness Rd, off Beach Rd, Bonnie Doon, East London, 5241
Tel: 043-735-3206 Fax: 043-735-3302
Email: nrainer@xsinet.co.za Web: www.loeriehide.co.za

The Loerie Hide has had a change of owners since our first edition but it has been a smooth transition. Nigel and Sue Rainer are an extremely hospitable couple, who clearly love their new home. I'm not surprised. East London has plenty of lush gardens (the Loerie Hide is no exception), but not many houses can boast direct access into a densely forested river valley. Like the brochure says, country living in the heart of East London. The garden plunges down to the Nahoon River and steep paths pick their way down through jungly vegetation. The trees of the valley are a natural aviary and if you're lucky, the flamboyant and lumbering loerie may be seen hopping around in the branches. Guests sleep in two rondavels (but three rooms) on a terrace cut into the slope and divided by a small pool (there is a fourth smaller room in the house). The styles are African (leopard and zebra skin prints, cane furniture) or rustic-cosy (brass bed, thatch, antiques, stone floor). The birds, meanwhile, get busy washing themselves in a bath made from an old grinding stone. Breakfast is served up on a wooden deck attached to the main house, where bougainvillea spills over the balcony and shade is provided by large umbrellas.

Rooms: 4: all doubles. All with en/s bathrooms, 3 with showers, 1 with a bath and a shower.
Price: R170 – R220 pp sharing. R220 – R275 singles.
Meals: Full breakfast included.
Directions: Ask for details when you book.

Umngazi River Bungalows

Terry and Tessa Bouwer
PO Box 75, Port St Johns, 5120
Tel: 047-564-1115 Fax: 047-564-1210
Email: umngazi@iafrica.com Web: www.umngazi.co.za

The wild coast may be South Africa's most spectacular, and yet least touristy region with its rock coastline, indigenous forests, secluded coves and many river mouths. And all this is on you doorstep at Umngazi, a lively family holiday resort where the only time you will spend indoor will be to sleep and eat. The relaxed and informal lodge is on the banks of the Umngazi estuar so you can choose between swimming in the pool, the river or the sea, fishing off rocks or boat: walking in the forests and horse-riding. Bird-watching cruises are also organised for sunset. Ferrie transport guests over to the beach from a river jetty. Meanwhile, back at home you will be missin out on tennis, snooker and table tennis. I guarantee that a week here, however lazy you are, w see the colour back in your cheeks and a bit of muscle on the arms and legs. And your sense o time will go haywire. Children are well catered for with trampoline, fort, sandpit, and designate dining room. You have a choice of sea-, river- or garden-facing cottages and there are thre honeymoon suites with working fireplaces, sliding doors onto private patios, sea views, a big sp bath and double outside shower. A beautiful spot where it's worth spending at least a few days

Rooms: 65 bungalows: twin or double on request, all have en/s bathrooms, most with baths and showers.
Price: From R290 to R425 pp sharing all-inclusive.
Meals: Breakfast, lunch and dinner included in the price (but not drinks.)
Directions: From the south, Umngazi lies 90 km due east of Umtata. From the north, via Flagstaff and Lusikisiki to Port St Johns on a mostly tarred road. There is also a transfer service from Umtata and a private flight service between Durban and Port St Johns.

Leliekloof Valley of Art

Dries and Minnie De Klerk
Burgersdorp, 9744
Tel: 051-653-1240 Fax: 051-653-1240
Email: sanart@intekom.co.za

What a place! Magnificent Bushman art and high-altitude wilderness to nourish the soul; log fires and home-cooked meals to look after earthier parts. Dries and Minnie have landed on their feet at Leliekloof, a farm adjoining their own property which they acquired a few years ago. The river here has chiselled a tortuous gorge through the sandstone and ironstone hills and the many caves host thirteen remarkable sites of Bushman art, many of the paintings of indeterminable age. Dries took me for an exhilarating morning drive and we visited two of them, Eland and Dog Caves. The quality of the paintings is superb, Dries a full reservoir of information about both the images and their artists. There is also a two-day scenic 19-kilometre hike around the valley, and a large dam for canoeing and trout fishing. Art apart, the countryside will extract from you superlatives you never knew you had. Single guests usually stay, for reasons of sociability, at the De Klerks' farm, while others have the run of Leliekloof House nearer the valley. The magnificent main room is 22 metres long, with sitting area, yellowwood bar, fireplace and huge antique Oregon pine dining table. You can self-cater, but given the stellar quality of Minnie's food (and the variety of things to do), I strongly suggest that you ask her to prepare your meals. Two nights minimum stay recommended.

Rooms: 1 farmhouse with 3 bedrooms (2 dbl and 1 twin, 2 with en suite bath, 1 en/s shower) plus loft sleeping 4; also 1 extra bathroom with bath & shower.
Price: Full board rates: R380 – R420 (for three or more). R400 – R440 for 2 people. Single rates on request.
Meals: Breakfast, lunch and dinner included. Dinner is 3 courses including bottle of wine.
Directions: 6 km south of Jamestown on N6 turn towards Burgersdorp. Turn right after 10 km. After another 5.5 km fork right and Leliekloof is another 1 km. Map can be faxed.

Die Tuishuise

Sandra Antrobus
36 Market St, Cradock, 5880
Tel: 048-881-1322 Fax: 048-881-5388
Email: tuishuise@eastcape.net Web: www.tuishuise.co.za

Unique accommodation indeed! Sandra has a raptor's eye for historic detail, laced with an antique dealer's nose and the heart of an interior designer – unparalleled in my experience of South Africa. There are 20 houses along Market Street, all antiquely furnished to reflect different styles, eras and professions. The houses were once lived in by bank managers, teachers, wagon makers etc, and you step into their nineteenth-century shoes when you stay – although the bathrooms, perhaps, retain a little more modernity. Each house is an antique shop in its own right, but modern comforts include fans, heaters and fireplaces. I was lucky enough to visit them all and it is no exaggeration to say I was struck dumb – reason enough for Sandra to have gone to the effort (some might feel). The hotel, a Victorian manor at the end of the street, has a further 19 rooms similarly done out in the style of the time and sherry is served in the drawing room before buffet dinners (my Karoo lamb was delicious). Sandra and her daughter Cherie are dedicated to presenting South African history in a way you can touch and feel. They also have a Xhosa singing group (Sofunda) – ask in advance. *Closed Christmas Day.*

Rooms: 20 restored 19th-century houses, each rented out as one 'unit'. There is also a hotel.
Price: From R165 pp sharing. No single supplement.
Meals: Full breakfast included and served until 9 am. Lunch and dinner by prior arrangement.
Directions: Ask when booking.

Wheatlands

Diana and Arthur Short
Route R75, Graaff-Reinet, 6280
Tel: 049-891-0422 Fax: 049-891-0422
Cell: 082-414-6503

Although today it is a busy sheep station, Wheatlands was built on the profits of ostrich feathers in the 1920s – a so-called feather palace. The house mingles Cape Dutch and Edwardian styles and was designed by the architect and landscaper Charles Bridgeman. The façade is dominated by three extravagant gables, while an oxide-floored verandah with white pillars slides along the horizontal. Park your wagon (or whatever you are driving these days) in the huge sandy courtyard and enter a long, cool, wood-panelled hall, an instant pleasure as you leave the desert heat of the Karoo. It's an appropriate home for the piano, all the antique furniture and the Persian rugs. The corridors are lined with books, there is a snug for reading and guest bedrooms are not converted outhouses, but an integral, lived-in part of the house. There are wonderful wanders to be had in a revelation of a back garden – lush and green with heritage roses growing like weeds. Diana and Arthur are astoundingly nice people, brimful of the hostly arts. Diana cooks delicious dinners, which are eaten at one large oak table. Arthur, meanwhile, is a serious farmer and cricketer… they even have their own ground.

Rooms: 3: all twins, 2 with en/s bathrooms with baths and showers, 1 with private bathroom with bath.
Price: R250 – R280 pp sharing.
Meals: Full breakfast and dinner included (Karoo lamb a speciality).
Directions: 42 km on the R75 south of Graaff-Reinet – Wheatlands turn-off to the left, 8 km up a gravel road.

DONKIN STREET

Cypress Cottage

Hillary Palmé

80 Donkin St, Graaff-Reinet, 6280
Tel: 049-892-3965 Fax: 049-892-3965
Email: info@cypresscottage.co.za Web: www.cypresscottage.co.za
Cell: 083-456-1795

Everyone from Greenwood Guides has now been to stay at Cypress Cottage and it is a pleasure to recommend it to you too. After a hot – and possibly bothersome – drive to this historic Karoo town, it is an immense relief to be welcomed by people as easy-going and instantly likeable as the Palmés and to be installed in a beautiful early 1800s Cape Dutch cottage… and to find yourself minutes later, cold beer in hand, on a stoep with magnificent mountain views. The bedrooms in the cottage are understatedly decorated with a (highly developed) taste for the natural and comfortable, thus the high reed ceilings, solid pine and slate floors, antique chests, fresh flowers and free-standing baths. Breakfast is laid up outside on the terrace – free-range eggs from house chickens, succulent figs, peaches, prunes and apricots from the orchards. Everything is as fresh and natural as possible. Guests can swim in the bore-hole fed reservoir, which has been converted into a swimming pool. The garden is an extraordinary feat of will and clever engineering – Hillary has managed to turn desert into lush vegetation despite the difficulties of brackish water. Graaff-Reinet is worth at least two days stopover in my opinion – Cypress Cottage many more.

Rooms: 3: 2 doubles and 1 twin. All with en/s bathrooms, 1 with bath, 1 with shower, 1 with both. All with aircon and heating!
Price: R180 – R250 pp sharing. Singles on request.
Meals: Full breakfast included.
Directions: From South: enter the town and pass the police academy on L and go over bridge. Two filling stations on L – take the road between them (West St). Follow to the very end, turn R into Donkin St, guest house first on L. From North: R at T-jct (Caledon St). 4th Left is Donkin St. House last on R.

KwaZulu Natal

Ivory Beach Lodge "The Cottage"

Massimo and Nicci Negra
379/1 Outlook Road, Southbroom, 4277
Tel: 039-316-8411 Fax: 039-316-8411
Email: masniki@venturenet.co.za Web: www.ivorybeachlodge.co.za
Cell: 082-440-9489 or 082-331-3202

Ivory Beach Lodge was not fully completed when Greenwood Guides visited last time, but it is now, and looks fabulous. So fabulous in fact that Massimo and Nicci have moved in themselves. That's where the bad news ends, however, as "The Cottage" can still be rented – in quotation marks, I can only presume, to highlight the shortcomings of the word in describing a place like this. A flight of steps beside the house takes you up through lush vegetation into blissful seclusion. The cottage shares all the features that make the main house so special. The style is Indo-African with high thatched ceilings, rough walls and pigmented floors, a well-equipped kitchen, inviting bedrooms and a very large, open-plan living area. There is also a deck surrounding the cottage with views over the white lines of surf pounding the beach. Less than a minute's walk through indigenous dune flora, past the 5th tee will get you there (you hardly notice it, but the property backs onto one of the golf coast's best courses). The Negras' award-winning trattoria, La Terrazza, is just 800 metres down the road on the edge of a sleepy lagoon. The obvious place to eat. *Booking essential. Breakfast by arrangement.*

Rooms: 1 cottage: 2 bedrooms with bathroom with double shower. Fully equipped kitchen for self-catering and a sitting room.
Price: The cottage is R400 – R500 pp sharing, Children half price.
Meals: Breakfast can be provided by arrangement and is not included in the price. The Negra's restaurant is 800m away for lunches and dinners!
Directions: Take the N3, the main toll-road travelling south. Exit at Southbroom South, travel 400 metres, turn first right into Outlook Road, and follow for 2 km (approx). You will see the lodge on your left, down a panhandle driveway.

KwaZulu Natal

123

Map Number 6

Figtree Lodge

Paul and Barbara Reynolds

30 North Ridge Road, Southbroom, 4277
Tel: 039-316-6547 or 082-421-1172 Fax: 039-316-8211
Email: sbelite@lantic.co.za Web: www.figtreelodge.co.za
Cell: 082-413-2955

Figtree Lodge is a trio of lodgings, all of which can be 'B&Bed' or self-catered. There's 'Figtree Loft', whose garden is home to the vast fig tree of the title. The tree's canopy is a magnet for hungry hadedahs, woodpeckers and purple-crested loeries and acts as a natural parasol when taking a leisurely lunch on the upstairs deck. The flat itself has an open-plan sitting-room and kitchen area, with a well-stocked 'honesty' fridge, and feels more like a home than a holiday flat, given the comfort levels and details like the well-thumbed paperbacks on the bookshelves. Over the road is the Reynolds' own house, with 'Kingfisher' attached, which comes with its own kitchen, lounge and beautiful photographic prints of wildlife on their old farm. Finally 'Swallow's Nest' is the large family house next door with a big garden and great views up the Imbezane River. I had a long chatty breakfast with Paul and Barbara in their dining room, but you can also have it 'at home' if you wish. Afterwards, their three border collies took Paul and myself for a walk on long deserted beaches. Bring your binoculars (whales go by from May to October) and leave your watch behind. *Self-catering also available in all the accommodation.*

Rooms: Figtree Loft – 3 rooms, 2 bathrooms (1 is en/s). "Kingfisher"; 1 room with en/s bathroom and sitting room. "Swallow's Nest"; 3 bedrooms, 2 bathrooms.
Price: B&B R195 – R250 pp sharing. Singles + R50. Self-catering prices on request.
Meals: Full breakfast included. There are 2 very good restaurants nearby.
Directions: Faxed or emailed when you book.

Ironwood Lodge

Jim Keightley
7 Figtree Lane, Pennington, 1484
Tel: 039-975-1895 Fax: 039-975-3895
Email: ironwood@scottburgh.co.za Web: www.ironwood.co.za

As I parked my car below the garden and walked up the steps (old ironwood railway sleepers) to the house, I was met by a barefoot man lightly sprinkled with dust, who introduced himself as Jim. Jim had taken advantage of a few precious moments of guestlessness to finish making a set of chairs, and as a thoroughly impractical person myself, I was drawn to all this hands-on know-how. It turns out that Jim is one of those polymath South Africans with umpteen strings to his bow. He has been in turn a fisherman, geography teacher and cabinet-maker. He does most things around Ironwood Lodge himself, from picking mussels off the beach and cooking them (or if not mussels then other fresh seafood), to building irrigation channels taking rainwater to his veggies, and making the furniture for the terrace. This is generally where meals are served, often by Jim and Caron's two children, Clinton and Warren, who clearly enjoy taking turns as head waiter. The view across the lush garden and out to sea is shared by the six large bedrooms, which come with their own garden or terrace upstairs. The beach is just over the road, and golf courses proliferate in the area. A very relaxed vibe.

Rooms: 6: 4 doubles, 2 twins all with en/s bathrooms; 2 with bath, 4 with showers.
Price: R195 – R295 pp sharing. Singles on request.
Meals: Full breakfast included. Dinner from R42.
Directions: From Durban take N2 to Pennington off-ramp. Follow signals to Pennington on R102 going south. Take left into Pennington, drive down to end and shopping complex. Left into Impathie Rd about 800 metres left into Figtree Lane.

Rosetta House

Bill & Lee McGaw

126 Rosetta Road, Morningside, Durban, 4001
Tel: 031-303-6180 Fax: 031-303-6180
Email: info@rosettahouse.com Web: www.rosettahouse.com
Cell: 082-447-6689

I can't describe Rosetta House as an urban oasis, for all its verdant credentials, as the whole neighbourhood is a symphony in green; but I can certainly give it both thumbs up. Lee used to travel as a medical rep, and is therefore expert at second-guessing those small but vital items you have left behind and providing them for you. The house has a big sitting room opening through to the dining area and the kitchen, where Lee prepares her heavenly breakfasts. On fine days you will have it out on the terrace, overlooking the lush, immaculate garden, whose four tall sentinel-like palms are frequently visited by a family of hadedahs, and the sea beyond. I whiled away a few idle moments looking out past King's Park rugby stadium and wondering where that ship in the bay was going (I eventually realised it was anchored, so not far was the answer). There's one room below the terrace, one inside and two others along the railway-sleeper path that crosses the garden. These have their own terrace and kitchen if rented together – but all the rooms are lovely. As a town house you will be grateful for all the convenient extras such as aircon, laundry, phone/fax/internet connection, safety deposit box, secure parking… and for the proximity of Rosetta to shopping, beaches and sports venues.

Rooms: 4: 1 double en/s shower in the house; 2 garden rooms sharing a kitchen (1 twin and 1 double, 1 en/s shower, 1 en/s bath); 1 double en/s shower.
Price: R225 – R250 pp sharing. Singles R325 – R350.
Meals: Full breakfast included. Close to some 30 restaurants for other meals.
Directions: Faxed when booking.

20 Palm Grove

Dallas and Rosemary Reed

cnr. 20 Palm Grove and 367 Ridge Rd, Berea, Durban, 4001
Tel: 031-208-5746 Fax: 031-208-5746
Email: enquiries@20palmgrove.co.za Web: www.20palmgrove.co.za
Cell: 082-442-7091

Once you park your car in your own lock-up garage you are ensconced in 20 Palm Grove's precincts, and Durban is elsewhere. Two of the guest rooms are in pretty cottages at the other end of the garden, beyond the pool and up sleeper-wood steps. They have their own sitting room with wicker chairs and TV, carpeted bedrooms and excellent showers, with soaps and shampoos provided, and both have a kitchen area. The third room is in the house and is very much a suite – with bathroom and sitting room (or it can be used as an extra single room) with all mod cons. The fourth, in an annexe to the house, is a bedroom with bathroom and has a private entrance. You can be as independent as you want, but Dallas and Rosemary certainly do not shy away from communing with their guests. You are welcome in the main house (1912), welcome to use the pool, and the Reeds will help you orientate yourself, recommend local eateries for dinner etc. Palm Grove is a family home in a quiet and fashionable part of town, ten minutes from the beaches, the city centre, several sports grounds and twenty minutes from the airport.

Rooms: 4: 3 twins/doubles (1 with extra single) with en suite shower rooms; 1 twin/double en/s bath and shower.
Price: R280 – R340 pp sharing. Singles R190 – R230.
Meals: Full breakfast included and served till 9 a.m.
Directions: Ask when booking.

Nalson's View

Wendy and Kelvin Nalson

10 Fairway Drive, Salt Rock
Tel: 032-525-5726 Fax: 032-525-5726
Email: nalsonsview@3i.co.za
Cell: 083-303-1533

After a long, long (long, long) day on the road I finally emerged from my car at Nalson's, wild-eyed and mud-besmattered. I couldn't have pitched up anywhere more perfect. Kelvin and Wendy welcomed me as if I had been living there for years. This was my room, these my beers and friends… I owned the place didn't I? A fantastic shower washed off the mud (don't ask) and I was invited to dinner. I couldn't tell who were guests, who were family friends, such is the open-house air of friendship here, and the meal was out of this world. Kelvin and Wendy have an oyster and mussel licence (guests can go with them and pick their own) and these were by FAR the best I've had in SA. Nalson's is one of those places where guests stop over for one night and have to be prised out of the place days later. Breakfast was sensational (both local baker and butcher are true servants of the community!) and, joy oh joy, freshly squeezed fruit juice. Guests who make the correct decision to stay more than one night will get involved in the sea activities – dolphin- and whale-watching on boats, fishing, bird-watching and the ten kilometres of beautiful Christmas Bay Beach. *Ask about children.*

Rooms: 4: 2 doubles, 1 family and 1 double/twin; 3 with en/s shower, 1 with en/s bath and shower.
Price: From R220 pp sharing. Singles R250.
Meals: Full breakfast included and served when you want it. Dinners by prior arrangement. Price depends on what you have.
Directions: From Durban take N2 north. Take exit 214 (Salt Rock/Umhlali). Right at T-junction signed to Salt Rock, follow road round to the right past Salt Rock Hotel (on your left). Fairway Drive is next right.

Seaforth Farm

Trevor and Sharneen Thompson
Exit 214 off N2, Salt Rock, Umhlali, 4390
Tel: 032-525-5217 Fax: 032-525-4495
Email: ttastym@iafrica.com Web: www.seaforth.co.za
Cell: 082-770-8376

Seaforth Farm is a full-bloom, vibrant, out-and-out treat of a guest house. Trevor and Sharneen have so many interests, talents and motivations that Seaforth is a constant source of stimulation. Sharneen is a water-colourist and has also won medals for flower-arranging, so the house blooms with ambitious and extravagant floral displays and paintings. Much of the furniture, made from teak, mahogany and oak is designed and crafted by Trevor in his workshop (his latest piece, a huge bed, adds lychee-wood to the repertoire), including inlays – and it is highly accomplished work. Then there is the lush garden, where the colour continues – look out for the 'queen of the night' cactus near the pool, with huge flowers that only open at night. Further afield are the Brahman cattle, the chickens, the pawpaw and pecan trees, the dam and its abundant birdlife. Trevor is coaxing it in with cunning plantation of pond weeds, lilies and islets, and you can bird-watch from a hide overlooking the dam. The guest house provides large, well-equipped bedrooms and a pool with dam-view deck for heavenly breakfasts cooked by Miriam Nkhomo, their long-standing housekeeper. Finally, the staff at Seaforth have a stake in the success of the venture. A pioneering guest house indeed....

Rooms: 4: 1 family cottage with 2 bedrooms, each with en suite shower; 2 doubles and 1 twin with en/s shower and bath.
Price: From R240 pp sharing. Singles from R300. Family suite from R495.
Meals: Full breakfast included. Romantic candle-lit curry evenings by arrangement from R75.
Directions: From Durban take the N2 north. Exit on the 214 signed Salt Rock. Go 200 metres and take the 1st right into Old Fort Road, then 1st left into Seaforth Ave – the house is at the end.

Fairlight B&B

Bruce and Michele Deeb

1 Margaret Bacon Avenue, (Corner South Beach Rd), Umdloti Beach, 4350
Tel: 031-568-1835 Fax: 031-568-1835
Email: enquiries@fairlight.co.za Web: www.fairlight.co.za
Cell: 082-443-8529

I got my first taste of Bruce and Michele's laid-back hospitality as soon as I arrived. It was another hot KwaZulu-Natal day, and I was bustled off for a much-needed dip in the sea across the road – "We can talk later". And we did. This newly-refreshed 'inspector' was soon sipping a cold beer by the pool and tucking into some delicious Lebanese pastries and thoroughly South African boerewors as Bruce tended the braai. The garden behind the house is dominated by two large milkwoods, a great place to shelter from the sun's glare during the day, although there are also sun-loungers around the pool. The front of the house has a wooden deck running all along it, from where you can watch the surfers – all the rooms open out onto it. Inside, it is effectively a family home (though four of the five kids have now moved out) and luxury guest house rolled into one – plenty of comfy spaces, family snaps on the wall and a warm, welcoming vibe to it. Rays of positive energy emanate from Michele and Bruce and their long-standing housekeeper Maria. Soak it up, then go forth and fish, surf or swim with a big smile on your face.

Rooms: 5: all sea-facing with en suite shower (2 with bath and shower).
Price: R280 – R400 pp sharing. Singles + 50%.
Meals: Full breakfast included. Dinners by request from R100 pp.
Directions: N2 exit to Umdloti. Follow down to roundabout. Keep right past Total garage and Fairlight is 500 metres along Beach Rd.

The Chase

Jane and Jonathan Chennells

PO Box 45, Eshowe, 3815
Tel: 035-474-5491 Fax: 035-474-1311
Email: thechase@netactive.co.za
Cell: 083-265-9629

Jane and Jonathan have so much to offer their guests that you hardly have to leave the premises. The weather-boarded house is gargantuan (Mrs Chennells senior had a penchant for large, open spaces) with long views of the farm's sugar cane plantations on overlapping mounds of distant hills. On clear days you can even see 90 degrees of sea. (They also have ducks, chickens, horses, cows, sheep and goats like a proper farm should, of course.) The garden is an orgy of barely controllable tropical growth, lush and colourful (check out the tulip tree and the Indian mahogany), its trees often weighed down by parasitic ferns and creepers. Birds are equally irrepressible and there are 70 species in the garden and 280 (!) in the Eshowe area. Kids will love the walled-in swimming pool (13 metres long) where you can swim by floodlight at night too. A hammock swings from a tree, a trampoline is stretched at ground level and there is a hard tennis court. Chennells Chase is an involving, very comfortable, incredibly good-value family home, with huge amounts of space inside and out. Pack a sense of humour and a pair of binoculars.

Rooms: 2: 1 twin, 1 double: 1 with en/s bath; 1 with private shower. Also a self-contained farm cottage with 5 beds at R400 per night.
Price: R180 pp sharing. Singles R250.
Meals: Full breakfast included (except in the cottage – by arrangement only) and served any time.
Directions: From Durban take N2 north for 1 hour. Turn off at Dokodweni off-ramp. Half an hour to Eshowe. Take first left signed to Eshowe, house 1.8 km signed on left.

Wendy's Country Lodge

Tony and Wendy Udal
3 Riverview Drive,
Riverview, Mtubatuba,
3935
Tel: 035-550-0407
Fax: 035-550-1527
Email:
wendybnb@iafrica.co.za
Web:
www.wendybnb.co.za
Cell: 083-628-1601

Tony and Wendy put their hearts into looking after their guests and this is an excellent-value spot from which to visit the nearby St Lucia Wetlands and Umfolozi Hluhluwe Game Park. The house is safely tucked away in a secure village and surrounded by the Udals' pride and joy, a full acre of tropical garden with pawpaw trees, anthuriums, and an orchid collection under cover in a 'cool house'. The bedrooms once belonged to children who have grown up and flown the nest and they have been converted, with twists of luxury, for guests. The biggest room was my favourite with its free-standing bath and shower, but all the rooms have aircon, bathrobes, mosquito nets, duvets in gingham covers and there's plenty of antiquity in the furniture too: old military trunks, early nineteenth-century Scottish pieces and a particularly nice breakfast table. You can swim in the heated pool, have a braai with the Udals or bird-watch in the amazing garden. Wendy and Tony are huge Natal enthusiasts and will make sure you get the most from your stay.

Rooms: 6: 3 twins, 3 doubles.
Price: R195 – R350 pp sharing. Singles on request.
Meals: Full breakfast included and served until 9 am. (Must vacate rooms by 10 am). Dinners by arrangement: R50 – R100. Country Club close by.
Directions: From Durban take the N2 north to Mtubatuba turn – follow to the T-junction. Go right where you'll see a sign to Wendy's and follow the signs to the house.

KwaZulu Natal

Hluhluwe River Lodge

Gavin and Bridget Dickson

Greater St Lucia Wetlands Park, Hluhluwe, 3960
Tel: 035-562-0246/7
Fax: 035-562-0248
Email: info@hluhluwe.co.za
Web: www.hluhluwe.co.za

A short drive through dense bushveld takes you to this friendly lodge on the shores of the Greater St Lucia Wetland Park. I suggest dropping things off in your wood-and-thatch chalet and making your way to the big deck, the centrepiece of the lodge, for a drink and some orientation. The view is straight across the Hluhluwe River flood plain. There is a pool lost in the trees near the Zulu boma (for evening braais), but most will want to make full use of the all-seeing, all-knowing guides (including Gavin himself) who will take you exploring in this remarkable region. The river is just there for canoe safaris in the channels and boat trips on the lake. Then there are game drives in luxury game-viewing vehicles through the sand forests or surrounding game parks (Hluhluwe Umfolozi Park and St Lucia). You can also go on botanical trips, or guided walks to old fossil banks and (astounding) bird-watching excursions in the park. Whatever you choose this is an intimate, sociable place, where small numbers and very knowledgeable guides make the experience personal and rewarding. The focus is on the topography, the birdlife and the wetland environment as a whole, rather than just the 'Big Five'.

Rooms: 12: 8 twins, 2 family rooms all with en suite shower; and 2 honeymoon suites with shower and bath.
Price: Dinner B&B R700 – R1195 pp sharing. Fully inclusive 2-night stay packages available.
Meals: Full board also includes 2 activities per day (boat trips, game drives, kayaking, forest walks and drives) .
Directions: From Durban take N2 to Hluhluwe. Turn off, go through town and follow signs to Mbazwane. 15 km on right-hand side is turn-off. 5 more km of dirt track.

Makakatana Bay Lodge

Hugh and Leigh-Ann Morrison
Mtubatuba, 3935
Tel: 035-550-4189 Fax: 035-550-4198
Email: maklodge@iafrica.com Web: www.makakatana.co.za
Cell: 082-573-5641

Makakatana Bay Lodge is sensational and I can do little to improve on these photos, which do not lie. If only we had space for ten shots, to show you every aspect of the lodge: the gleaming wooden interiors; the bedrooms, connected by walkways through the forest, with their gargantuan slabs of glass and warm, earthy African colours; the pool encased in decking and raised above the grasses of the wetlands; the lake itself and the extraordinary St Lucia waterways. Guests are taken on pole-driven safaris in mokoro canoes, searching for birds (360 species!), crocodiles and hippos. You can also take a boat trip across the lake for lunch on the beach or a game drive to a nearby reserve before returning to a sumptuous dinner with your hosts in the outdoor boma. The family's old 'Crab House' is the only part of the lodge not raised above the tall grasses. This was once a storeroom for crabs caught in the lake, now a wine cellar with a giant tree growing out of its roof. Huge sliding doors throughout the lodge open onto wooden decks with views over the lake, and the absence of railings just adds to the feeling of openness to nature. From the wooden Swazi tortoise holding open the front door, Hugh and Leigh-Ann will have you hooked. The lodge is beautifully welded to its environment. An absolute treat.

Rooms: 5 rooms: 2 kings and 3 twins with en suite bath and outside shower.
Price: From R1795 pp sharing. From R2395 for singles.
Meals: Fully inclusive of all meals and safaris.
Directions: Take N2 north from Durban for 250 km to Charter's Creek. Follow road for 15 km (14 km on tar) to fork. Take right fork and follow signs to Makakatana Bay Lodge (4 more km or so).

Kosi Forest Lodge

Brett Gehren

Kosi Bay Nature Reserve, PO Box 1593, Eshowe, 3815
Tel: 011-463-3376 Fax: 011-463-3358
Email: info@zulunet.co.za Web: www.zulunet.co.za

Kosi Bay is the sort of place that novelists map out and then construct adventures in. You are picked up by a four-wheel drive, which can negotiate the sand tracks criss-crossing the region. You park up not just your car, but also the modern world you are now leaving. There is no tar and no electricity here. Instead you enter a landscape of raffia palm groves, primary sand forests, mangroves, water meadows, interconnecting lakes (yes hippo and crocodile like it too and are regularly sighted). And then there is the sea and the mouth of the river for diving, swimming and fishing in 'perfect white sand coves with huge overhanging trees' (says the lodge brochure). The reed-thatched camp itself perfectly balances the wild (your chalet is in the middle of a boisterous forest) with the romantic (candlelit meals and outdoor baths and showers). I loved the deep stillness of the early-morning guided canoe trip and other activities include reef snorkelling, turtle tracking, forest walks and bird safaris. I consider Kosi Forest Lodge one of the most rewarding (and therefore best-value) places I have stayed in SA. I recommend a minimum of two or three nights.

Rooms: 8: 1 family 'bush suite'; 6 twins and 1 honeymoon double; all with outdoor bath and shower.
Price: All-inclusive (meals and activities) R885 – R1045 pp sharing. Sing. supp. 30%. Transfer from police station R15 pp. Children under 12 half price.
Meals: All meals and teas included.
Directions: From Hluhluwe take N2 north past Mkuze. Turn R signed Jozini. In Jozini thru' town, L over the dam and follow for 37 km. Turn R at T-jct and follow for 67 km to Kwangwanase. R at Kosi Forest sign and follow tar road round to R and up slope to police station compound. Turn L and park under trees.

Map Number 13

Shayamoya Tiger Fishing and Game Lodge

Lindy Blevin
PO Box 784, Pongola, 3170
Tel: 034-435-1110 Fax: 034-435-1008
Email: shayalodge@saol.com Web: www.shayamoya.co.za
Cell: 083-456-8423

Shayamoya is family-run and has that edge of friendliness that can seem contrived elsewhere. The youthful energy that emanates from Lindy and the crew is contagious. Just as well. There is so much to do within the broad ambit of the Pongola Biosphere: game drives in 10,000 hectares of well-stocked park (with everything except lions and cheetahs), guided walks, river canoeing, mountain biking and elephant tracking (there is a herd of 38 animals). A highlight is the tiger fishing (big teeth, very feisty) on the vast dam, but you can also enjoy a more leisurely cruise up the river in search of crocs and hippos. The central deck at the lodge has a wild view over Pongolapoort Lake to the mountains and Swaziland beyond. This is the heart of the lodge, where meals are eaten, drinks knocked back and lies told after fishing expeditions. Nandie, a spotted eagle owl, often drops by and listens in. The chalets each have their own decks and cobbled outdoor showers and wooden wash stands inside hold pottered basins (with ceramic hippo plugs you won't see anywhere else). The whole place hums with the life of the surrounding wilderness. *Pool and boma for swims and braais.*

Rooms: 10: 8 chalets, each with private viewing deck, doubles/twins with en suite bath and outdoor shower. And 2 honeymoon suites.
Price: From R780 pp sharing, fully inclusive of all meals, teas, coffees and 1 activity per day, (but not tiger-fishing). R150 single supplement.
Meals: Full breakfast, light lunch and 4-course dinner included.
Directions: Shayamoya is 2 km off the N2 between Pongola (27 km) and Mkuze (40 km), on the road to Golela on the Swazi border.

Babanango Valley Lodge

John and Meryn Turner
Zululand, AngloZulu Battlefields, 3850
Tel: 035-835-0062 Fax: 035-835-0160
Email: bvlodge@mweb.co.za Web: www.babanangovalley.com

A twelve-kilometre driveway is like a red rag to the Greenwood Guide's bull, and once again a (slight, let's be honest) sense of adventure has been magnificently rewarded. A winding dirt road took me down into the beautiful Babanango Valley and John and Meryn Turner's secluded lodge, set in its own 8,000-acre nature reserve. John was born in Zululand and loved his indigenous plants even before getting his doctorate in ecology. He and Meryn are the friendliest, most considerate and unflappable hosts, and I loved my stay here. As is so often the case with more remote places, there is an abundance of things to do, and I left far too soon. Just taking in the views (or star-gazing at night) is fun, but you can also go for long walks along trails in the reserve and build up an appetite for a candlelit dinner amid scenes from the Anglo-Zulu war, another of John's passions. He often takes battlefield tours to Isandlwana and Rorke's Drift and the Zulu historical sites, and can also organise 'Big Five' game viewing in nearby Hluhluwe-Umfolozi game reserve. Stay at least two days. *The Turners also have a more rustic bush camp, 'Rock Pools'. Closed 24th – 26th December.*

Rooms: 8: 1 double, 7 twins; 7 with en/s bath and shower, 1 with shower only. There is also a bush camp, "Rock Pools".
Price: From R840 pp sharing (from R1090 for singles) for dinner, B&B. 'Rock Pools' from R420.
Meals: Lunches available R30 – R45 or included in guided tour. Dinner included.
Directions: Follow N2 north from Durban to Dokodweni off-ramp. Take R66 through Gingindlovu and Eshowe to Melmoth, then follow R68 to Babanango. 4 km beyond Babanango is the D139 on your right, as well as a signpost. Follow this road for 12 km and you are there.

Fugitives' Drift Lodge

David and Nicky Rattray
Rorke's Drift, 3016
Tel: 034-271-8051 Fax: 034-271-8053 or 034-642-1843
Email: fugdrift@trustnet.co.za Web: www.fugitives-drift-lodge.com
Cell: 034-642-1843

You don't have to know anything about the Anglo-Zulu war to enjoy the Fugitives' Drift experience. Most people who turn up there have seen the film *Zulu*, and half-remember the heroics. But David Rattray and his highly knowledgeable historians transform the portrayal of the Isandlwana and Rorke's Drift battles with theatrical expression. We sat on a hill, the battlefield spread below us, as our guide, with windmilling arms, wild eyes and occasional bouts of Zulu chanting, brought the scene to life for us. Vivid stuff and not found elsewhere. Dinner back at the lodge was terrific, the atmosphere built preprandially around an open fire where we guests sat in a semi-circle, introducing ourselves, nibbling on African style eats, and putting back a couple of beers. Stories flourished over dinner as wine, truly delicious food and candlelight worked their inevitable magic. Bedrooms are in separate cottages with large bathrooms and my deep bath after dinner was by the light of hurricane lamps. I did not meet the Rattrays when I visited (they were on holiday), but the experience was still a special one. Just down the road there is a cheaper alternative, The Guest House, also run by Fugitives.

Rooms: 8: all twins with bath and shower. 3 bedroom annexe cottage with 6 beds and 2 bathrooms.
Price: R920 – R1350 pp sharing. Singles R1250 – R1600. Cottage R525 for 3 or more.
Meals: Full breakfast, lunch and dinner included. Tours R495 pp.
Directions: From Durban take the N3 north to Pietermaritzburg. Exit onto R33 towards Greytown – follow signs to Dundee, through Keats Drift, Tugela Ferry and Pomeroy. 12 km after Pomeroy go right to Elandskraal, at Church turn left to Rorke's Drift – sign right to Fugitives' Drift on D31 (14 km).

Isibindi Zulu Lodge

Brett Gehren

Rorke's Drift, Dundee, 3000
Tel: 011-463-3376 Fax: 011-463-5308
Email: info@zulunet.co.za or isibindi@iafrica.com
Web: www.zulunet.co.za

As I drove up to Isibindi in the early evening, the way ahead was intermittently illuminated by a spectacular thunderstorm. It seemed to be following me. Ignoring the portents, I pressed on Homerically to claim my prize, a night at the wonderful (the first line of my notes just read 'Wow!') Isibindi Zulu Lodge. It sits on a hill in the middle of a 2000-hectare nature reserve on the Buffalo river, with six secluded chalets looking out over the bush, a modern spin on the traditional Zulu beehive hut. The best view is reserved for the swimming pool, a great place to unwind after an early game drive with lodge manager Dieter. He's a talking bush encyclopaedia and great barman (and it's a great bar – a hunk of polished acacia, with local animal species and a map of the battle of Isandlwana painted on the wall). He also provides an effective foil to resident Zulu historian Prince Sibusiso Zulu, whose cultural evenings combine education with fun (it is possible!) Prince also leads tours to the Anglo-Zulu war battlefields, which weave together dramatic tales from both sides. Isibindi has it all, nature, history, culture and even adrenaline sports – the rafting camp in the reserve is one of the best in South Africa.

Rooms: 6: 4 twins, 1 double, 1 honeymoon beehive suite; all with en suite bath and shower.
Price: R530 – R890 pp sharing. Single supp. 30%.
Meals: Full board includes breakfast, lunch and dinner, hikes and 1 game drive per day. Rafting, Zulu cultural evening and homestead visits extra.
Directions: Take R33 south from Dundee for 14 km, then turn left onto dirt road to Rorke's Drift – 25 km or so. Follow signs to Isibindi. 5 km beyond the village of Rorke's Drift.

139 Map Number 12

Mawelawela Game and Fishing Lodge

George and Herta Mitchell-Innes

Fodo Farm, PO Box 21, Elandslaagte, 2900
Tel: 036-421-1860 Fax: 036-421-1860
Email: mitchellinnes@mweb.co.za Web: www.skybusiness.com/mawelawela
Cell: 083-259-6394 or 082-734-3118

George and Herta are a natural, down-to-earth couple whose veins of hospitality run deep… and their farmhouse B&B is awash with incidental pleasures. Herta, a bubbly Austrian, moved out to South Africa twenty-seven years ago and married George, who is a beef farmer – his boerewors is delicious. He is also a keen historian, which explains the painting of an unhappy Napoleon on his way to St Helena which stares out at the family dining room, and all those history books that crowd the shelves at the end of the long table. George also has a study full of weighty tomes on the Anglo-Boer wars, including a fascinating London Illustrated News annual from 1899. I could have spent hours sitting among the prints of battle scenes. George often does, and he also leads tours out to the nearby battlefields, especially Elandslaagte. The two twin rooms at the end of the main house are both very comfortable, and the bungalow across the jacaranda-filled garden is perfect for a family or group. Beyond is the farm itself which, as well as the cattle, is home to several species of large antelope, a couple of trout dams and a steady flow of backpackers (there is also a hostel on the farm). *Self-catering also available in the bungalow.*

Rooms: 3 units: 2 twins; 1 with en/s bath, 1 with en/s bath and shower. 1 apartment with double, twins and single which can be self-catering or B&B.
Price: B&B: From R170 pp sharing.
Meals: Full breakfast included. 3-course dinner also available from R75.
Directions: On N11, 35 km from Ladysmith, 70 km from Newcastle. Also entrance on R602, 35 km from Dundee.

Oaklands Country Manor

Jamie and Anna Bruce
PO Box 19, Van Reenen, 3372
Tel: 058-671-0067 Fax: 058-671-0077
Email: oaklands@compuserve.com Web: www.oaklands.co.za
Cell: 083-304-2683

Jamie was in the British army for many years and memorabilia pops up at Oaklands in flags and prints. He also runs very popular tours to the nearby Boer War battlefields – but there is no regimentation at Oaklands. The colonial manor, with its original Oregon pine floors and ceilings, is now an intimate country hotel set in 260 acres of heavenly highveld countryside, once home to San tribesmen (see their rock paintings) and still the favoured beat for 185 species of bird. Back at the Manor, kids are well catered for (Jamie and Anna adore them): there's the balustraded pool and a tennis court (with umpire's chair to provoke argument), croquet, a games room, mountain bikes and all that fresh mountain air will put them to sleep should they ever sit down. The stone-walled rooms are fun, converted from old stables and outbuildings. All are different in style, but consistent themes are the colourful duvet covers, bright African art, and stunning views from the patios. You are out in the wilds here among mountains, craggy cliffs and paddocks full of galloping horses. The Oaklands pub is renowned for its warm atmosphere and meals, prepared by resident chef Tank, a monument to his own cooking, are superb to boot.

Rooms: 13: 7 twins, 6 doubles all with en/s baths and shower over the bath.
Price: R580 – R780 pp sharing. R610 – R860 for singles.
Meals: Full breakfast and dinner included. Lunch is also available.
Directions: Take the N3 to Van Reenen, turn right at the Caltex garage. Go 7 km down a dirt track – Oaklands is signed to the right.

Map Number 12

Wyford Farm

Sheila and Stratford Russell

PO Box 22, Van Reenen, 3372
Tel: 058-671-0025 Fax: 058-671-0025
Email: wyford@mweb.co.za
Web: www.guestnet.co.za/kz/wyford/wyford.htm   Cell: 072-149-0608

Built 120 years ago as a trading post on the busy Van Reenen Pass, Wyford is now a working farm a short drive off the new road – far enough, anyway, for time to stand still. Green fields stretch out and sporadic cattle contentedly chew the cud (at least they look content – who knows what they're really thinking?). This is a Mecca for kids with all those farm animals, the swimming pool, horse-riding and so much wide, open countryside. The family unit in the main house has a bathroom made completely of stone (the shower area is huge) and the cottages have little gardens and converted sleeping lofts under the thatch, always a popular option with children. Sheila has added a comfortable Zulu beehive hut since our last visit, but the gorgeous views up to the mountain pass remain immutable. Self-catering is possible, but I suggest a hearty breakfast (and home-cooked dinner if arranged in advance), not just for the food, but so you come into contact with Sheila, who is charming and down-to-earth. In fact, the whole farm is charming and down-to-earth. As is said so often in this book, you will regret booking in for one-night only. There is too much else to do.

Rooms: 4: 1 Zulu beehive hut and 3 cottages: Garden Cottage and old trading store is a double; Aloe is a twin with large sitting room; Poplar has 2 beds + large loft.
Price: R150 – R180 pp sharing. No single supplement.
Meals: Full breakfast included and lunches and dinners by arrangement. Dinner from R60. Self-catering also available.
Directions: Wyford is situated 9 km south of Van Reenen village and 1.8 km off the N3 between Harrismith and Ladysmith. Wyford Farm is clearly signed off the N3.

Three Tree Hill Lodge

Andrew Ardington
PO Box 3534, Ladysmith, 3370
Tel: 036-448-1171 Fax: 036-448-1953
Email: fugdrift@trustnet.co.za Web: www.threetreehill.co.za

This is the comfortable way to experience the Boer War and one of its most famous battlefields, Spionkop Hill. The lodge sits in complete isolation on an opposing hill with views that flood out across the green valley, and down to the Spionkop Nature Reserve. You can often see giraffe, zebra, rhino etc from the stoep, although at some distance. There is an all-together feeling at Three Tree Hill. Meals are eaten at one table and the atmosphere is involving on the tours. Andrew knows his potatoes when it comes to the history too – his Boer War tours are engrossing. Meanwhile, back at the lodge you can take time out from all the action in very private cottages, with their own unobserved verandah looking onto the park. They are simple in design with orange oxide floors, hand-embroidered covers on beds – the aloe is the house symbol – wooden wash stands in bathrooms, 100 per cent cotton sheets, down duvets for crisp winter nights. The emphasis is on simple good quality, rather than elaborate decoration. For me the *pièce de résistance* at the lodge was the swimming pool, reached through a gauntlet of dalek-like aloes, and perched precariously on the hip of the valley.

Rooms: 6: all twins all with en/s bathrooms with baths and showers.
Price: R750 – R900 pp sharing. Singles: R950 – R1200.
Meals: Full breakfast, lunch and dinner included. Tours of the battlefields for R320.
Directions: From Durban take the N3 north for 260 km – take the R616 left for 19 km towards Bergville. Go left onto the D564 for 8 km.

Old Rearsby Farm Cottages

Brigadier Jim and Jeannie Parker

Old Rearsby, Hlatikulu Rd, Mooi River, 3300
Tel: 033-263-2280 or 033-263-1331 Fax: 033-263-2475
Email: parker@parkertours.co.za Web: www.parkertours.co.za
Cell: 082-667-7755

I loomed out of the night – cold, wet and very late (sorry!) – but was still treated to the warmest of welcomes from the Parkers. This, as I understand it from a string of previous visitors, is typical at Old Rearsby (the welcome I mean). My flagging spirits were rekindled by a canny combination of single malt and human kindness, and we were soon chatting away in the drawing room among the water-colours and military prints (Jim was the British defence adviser in Pretoria until 1996, when the Parkers moved here). I eventually ambled back across the lawn to my cottage (one of three set a little apart from the main house), which comes with plenty of books and magazines to read and its own fireplace prepared for lighting. One deep slumber later the rain was a distant memory, and I opened my door to fabulous views across to the central Drakensberg mountains (it's phenomenal hiking country, so bring boots). Breakfast included fruits from the orchard at the back of the garden (peaches, plums and apricots), and I was on my way far too soon. A final smile on the way out – Jim has aligned the driveway to point directly at Giant's Castle peak. *The Parkers are also tour-brokers (see their website) by the way.*

Rooms: 3 cottages: All with twin rooms and with en/s bathrooms; 2 with showers, 1 with bath.
Price: R180 pp sharing. Singles on request.
Meals: Full breakfast included. Picnic lunch and dinner by arrangement.
Directions: Take either the Mooi River north or south ramp from the N3 and follow all Giant's Castle signs through and out of village. After climbing straight up Lawrence Rd for 2 km, take next left signed 'Hlatikulu 22'. Old Rearsby is another 5 km drive on the right.

Sewula Gorge Lodge

Graham & Santie McIntosh & Jacquie Geldart
Off R103, 18 km from Estcourt, Estcourt, 3310
Tel: 036-352-2485 Fax: 036-352-2868
Email: bookings@sewula.co.za Web: www.sewula.co.za
Cell: 082-824-0329

Take a glorious setting beside a waterfall in the middle of a nature reserve, add lashings of comfor (don't hold back, you can't overdo it), blend the mix into the natural environment and garnish with wildly original carpentry and sculpture by South African artist Bruce Attwood. *Et voilà*, the Sewula recipe! It is hassle-free, unless you particularly hate cooking, which will be your only mission (should you choose to accept it… and it's a wonderful kitchen too). Sewula's friendly staff will do the rest: wash up, tidy rooms twice a day, light fires, provide milk, cream, butter and firewood Each cottage has a different view from its balcony, and a sleeping loft for kids. The emphasis is on relaxation and seclusion – they don't book in more than one party at a time and staff live away from the lodge. You can swim in rock-pools, walk around the reserve on trails in search of it various antelope species and even immerse yourself in centuries of history, from iron-age settlements to Zulu-Boer battle memorials. A final word for lodge manager Jacquie Geldart whose constant thoughtfulness will have made your stay, often without your even noticing. It's self-catering, Jim, but not as we know it!

Rooms: 4 cottages: 8 adults and 10 children can be housed – or up to 13 single adults!

Price: Midweek from R250 self-catering. Weekends and holidays from R300. Children half-price if sleeping in loft.

Meals: Well-equipped kitchen for self-catering with milk, butter, cream, firewood inc. Breakfasts for R40 pp by prior arrangement. Restaurants nearby.

Directions: Exit 143 on N3 from Durban to Mooi River. Take R103 to Estcourt, 20.3 km from off-ramp, take right turn onto dirt road to Malanspruit and follow signs to Sewula Gorge Camp (5 km from turn-off to reception).

Stocklands Farm

Eve Mazery
4 Shafton Rd, Howick, 3290
Tel: 033-330-5225 Fax: 033-330-5225
Email: edulink@iafrica.com Web: www.stocklandsfarm.co.za
Cell: 082-975-2298

The warm welcome I received as I tumbled out of my car, late and weary, is undoubtedly typical of Stocklands. As my cognitive faculties jolted back into life over a restorative beverage, it became obvious that Eve and Roland are natural hosts, thoughtful, funny, relaxed. They have put a lot of love – Eve buys presents for the rooms whenever she goes away – and plenty of style into this wonderful old house. The argument goes that half-measures are not really in keeping with Stocklands, and you can see their point. The walls of the original 1850's house, for example, are over 50 centimetres thick and the Belhambra tree at the front of the house, a South American tree planted by early residents for shade, is no-less-than enormous. The four rooms are meticulously decorated to individual themes, their French names (Alouettes, Tournesols, etc – if you know a French bird that would cover 'waterfowl' then please let him know) hinting at Roland's Mauritian roots. They are full of incidental delights, such as blown-glass candle-holders from a trip to Finland, and little complimentary items for ablution or consumption. The cottages are very comfortable too, and all the accommodation benefits from the huge garden. *Game is to be viewed right next door by the way.*

Rooms: 4 en/s rooms – 2 suites & 2 bedrooms, 1 with en/s bath, 3 with en/s shower. 2 cottages: 1 w/ 3 bedrooms & 2 bathrooms, 1 w/ 2 bedrooms, 1 shower.
Price: R180 – R240 pp sharing. Self-catering from R75 – R140 depending on numbers.
Meals: Full breakfast included or you can self-cater in the cottages. The Mazerys will point you to excellent restaurants nearby.
Directions: From Jo'burg take N3 to Durban. Take first exit to Howick signed Howick/Tweedie. At Stop

sign turn left to Howick. Thru' lights to bottom of hill, turn left to Karkloof. 100m turn R into Shafton Rd. Stocklands is 1km. From Durban take N3 to Jo'burg. Take 3rd Howick turn-off as above.

Map Number 12

Kloof Falls Lodge

Gabriella and Anthony Elworthy

8 Umvemve Place, Kloof
Tel: 031-764-1502
Fax: 031-764-6209
Email:
gabriella@klooffallslodge.co.
Web:
www.klooffallslodge.co.za

As I sat down to a refreshing drink and a chat on the terrace with Gabriella and Anthony, it took me a few moments to adjust to my surroundings. I had been in the middle of Durban 20 minutes earlier, and now I was overlooking a deep gorge and the series of waterfalls from which this delightful place takes its name. You are close to nature here: a gate at the end of the Elworthys steep terraced garden takes you into the Krantzkloof nature reserve and a whole series of trails leading down into the gorge where duiker, bushbuck and skittish monkeys lurk. The valley also has a breeding pair of crowned eagles (preferred diet: monkeys), which nest nearby and regularly come and perch in the garden's flat crown trees. Bird-watchers will be kept busy. The lodge is also Gabriella and Anthony's home, but guests have their own living room (bright, airy, full of books and with a hi-fi and TV) and terrace. The bedrooms are all very comfortable and Gabriella's breakfasts delicious. There really is no catch. The Elworthys are great hosts and great fun… and to cap it all Anthony is a tea trader by profession. I haven't had a better cuppa in South Africa.

Rooms: 4: 3 doubles, 1 single – 2 twins with en/s showers; 1 double with private bathroom, bath and shower; the single has en/s shower.
Price: From R175 pp sharing. From R215 single.
Meals: Full breakfast included. There are lots of restaurants nearby.
Directions: M13 from Durban, exit 23 – follow M33W signs, past Kloof Mall, over railway bridge, left into Church Road. At T-jct turn right and follow road past the civic offices and schools. Kloof Falls Lodge signs will guide you to Umvemve Place – number 8 is on the left-hand side.

Penwarn Country Lodge

Peta Parker

PO Box 253, Southern Drakensberg, Underberg, 3257
Tel: 033-701-1777 or 1341 or 1342 Fax: 033-701-1341 or 417
Email: ppp@futurenet.co.za Web: www.penwarn.com
Cell: 083-305-3009

Sam gave Penwarn a rave write-up in the first edition, and I can see no reason to change the tune. It is simply fantastic! The more adventurous will sleep in a cave with its own bushman painting, its own dam (frothing with trout) and a bath hewn from natural rock. Since our last visit a magnificent stone lodge has been added, complete with decking overlooking the main dam and the mountains beyond. But you can still stay in a secluded cypress log cabin or at the main lodge, converted from an old sandstone dairy and fertilizer shed into luxurious bedrooms. The list of things to do at Penwarn is exhaustive (and exhausting!): trout-fishing on dams and rivers (lessons and rods provided); riding (which I can highly recommend); tubing on fast-flowing rivers, hiking in beautiful scenery, with the southern Drakensberg as a backdrop, bird-watching (lammergeyers may join you at the Vulture Restaurant), mountaineering or abseiling (tricky cliffs are everywhere), and game drives (tame eland will approach you). Some find it all so exciting they get married by a dam in front of the lodge! Peta and Bruce are great fun, and their boundless energy keeps it all running smoothly. Finally a mention for Nimrod, a tame otter partial to sausages, and Jonty, more pussycat than caracal. *Clay-pigeon shooting and archery also available.*

Rooms: 13: 7 double rooms in the main Indabushe lodge, 4 rooms in Mthini lodge, 1 cave. All with en/s bathrooms.
Price: From R570 – R650 full board pp sharing. R100 single supplement. From R170 self-catering in cave and cabin.
Meals: Full breakfast, lunch and dinner included.
Directions: Take Exit 99 off N3 marked Underberg, Howick South and travel 110 km west to Underberg, going through Boston and Bulmer en route. Take the Swartberg Road out of Underberg
and after 5 km turn right onto Bushman's Neck Road (dirt track). After 16 km turn L to Penwarn (drive is 4 km long.)

Free State & Lesotho

Smithfield House

Graeme Wedgwood

Brand St, Smithfield, 9966
Tel: 051-683-0071 Fax: 051-683-0045
Email: smithfieldho@icon.co.za Web: www.smithfieldhouse.cjb.net
Cell: 082-450-6779

Those with a taste for fine living will find a kindred spirit in Graeme, a man whose love of house and garden, countryside, good company, food and wine sets the tone at Smithfield House. He was once a gallery owner in Johannesburg – a far cry from his first, 26-year career as a London stockbroker – and his personal art collection enriches the walls of this 1880s colonial mansion. There's a rather 'racy' Battiss and a more demure Elizabeth Frink, while several works by South African artists, of which Graeme is particularly proud, form a gauntlet down the pine-floored central corridor. High ceilings throughout keep the interior cool in summer and open fires make for cosiness in winter. The bath towels are thick, bed linen crisp and more examples of the house art collection dot the bedroom walls. Seven acres of gardens and grounds are surrounded by tall trees (Graeme has planted more than 200), shading well-tended lawns and neat flowerbeds. There is an intriguing L-shaped swimming pool and an all-weather tennis court too. Smithfield House is a bastion of stylish living and since the first edition a number of travel magazines have paid homage to the mercurial delights on offer. *Graeme will explain about horse-riding, hill-climbing, game viewing, sailing on the Gariep Dam, Caledon River fishing etc.*

Rooms: 3: 1 double, 2 twins all with en/s bathrooms, 2 with showers and 1 with a bath and shower.
Price: R180 – R220 pp sharing. Single supplement available on request
Meals: Full breakfast included and dinners by *special* arrangement.
Directions: There are two huge signs to Smithfield House in town and it's a very small town. You can't miss it.

Pula House

Barbara and John von Ahlefeldt

PO Box 88, Smithfield, 9966
Tel: 051-683-0032 Fax: 051-683-0032
Email: pula@acenet.co.za Web: www.pula-house.com
Cell: 083-272-3001

Sophistication and jaunty modernity mix eclectically and effectively in this Karoo-style house. It was built over 120 years ago for the local magistrate but was sadly neglected before journalists John and Barbara retired from their Devonshire inns in England and got their hands on it. Life has now been breathed back into the old place, and with interest. Exotic rugs and pine floors are separated from 15-foot-high pressed metal ceilings by brightly coloured walls; original South African art and conservative hunting prints hang peaceably next to a highly decorative carpet coat – a relic of 60s London; handsome antique furniture enjoys the presence of modern Africana. 'Juxtaposition' is a word that keeps coming to mind. With precious little water (this is the Karoo after all), Barbara has worked a minor miracle with lush lawns, interesting nooks and crannies to explore, rashes of vivid colour in the garden, and the quirky plunge pool is a summer godsend. The sun disappears behind a koppie and sunset on the terrace is a special time at Pula. Finally von Ahlefeldt hospitality is second to none (a matter of pride at Pula House) and the home-made breads and creamy scrambled eggs make breakfasts truly excellent.

Rooms: 4: 2 doubles, 2 twins all with en/s bathrooms, 2 with baths, 2 with showers.
Price: R180 – R220 pp sharing. Single supplement R60.
Meals: Full breakfast included.
Directions: Pula House is on Douglas Street which comes off the N6 directly opposite the police station on the Bloemfontein side of town.

Bishop's Glen

Ted and Bits Quin
PO Box 9, Glen, 9360
Tel: 051-861-2210 Fax: 051-861-2210
Email: bishopsglen@connix.co.za

It's a particular pleasure to stay in a place where the owners give of themselves as unstintingly as Ted and Bits do. I love the fact that they join you (you join them?) for both dinner and breakfast – this is what staying in somebody's home is all about. Nine of us sat down to a sumptuous dinner in the evening and added new resonance to the word 'convivial'. The house dates back to 1813, and the dining room still has some of the original yellowwood timbers. All is lived-in yet elegant, with beautiful wooden furniture and family portraits in abundance. Earlier we had gathered on the plant-encrusted verandah, looking out over the lush garden and its 200-plus bird species, before moving to the sitting room where Ted's 27 (I counted) cattle trophies fill up one wall. My bedroom was impressively large and timbered, with pretty linen and a substantial array of novels. No old travel magazines here! Bits (a childhood friend called Pieces is out there somewhere) does not take last-minute bookings – she likes to be prepared – so make sure you ring well in advance to reserve a night in one of the Free State's finest, homeliest bolt-holes. *There is also a game farm, with many different antelopes.*

Rooms: 3: 1 double and 2 twins; all with en suite shower, 1 with shower and bath.
Price: Dinner bed and breakfast: R250 – R300 pp sharing. Singles R325 – R375.
Meals: Full breakfast included. Also dinner: 3 courses with pre-dinner drinks and wine at table.
Directions: Faxed or emailed on booking. Glen is 20 km north of Bloemfontein.

Malealea Lodge and Pony Trek Centre

Mick and Di Jones

Malealea, Lesotho
Tel: 051-447-3200 Fax: 051-448-3001
Email: malealea@mweb.co.za Web: www.malealea.co.LS
Cell: 082-552-4215

You shouldn't need an excuse to go to the kingdom of Lesotho, but if you do, look no further than Malealea Lodge. Here in the country's heartland – no phones, no mains electricity – Mick and Di have created a fascinating environment through a combination of their own personal warmth, native knowledge and a wealth of natural and cultural attractions. Malealea thrives on its interaction with the neighbouring village, but this is no plasticky 'Cultural Village' experience. The lodge is entered via the area's trading station, horses for treks of up to six days are hired locally and children will guide you on hikes. In the evenings, you listen to a local choir, before a band plays with home-made instruments. It's worth travelling off the high roads to experience moments such as these! Communal suppers are served canteen style – backpackers and ambassadors rub comradely shoulders – before the pub and firelit stoep drag you away. Later your torch guides you back to thatched rondavel or farmhouse-style accommodation – try to stay as near to the front as possible. I arrived in the afternoon rain but woke up to the most stunning of mornings, with the mist lying low down in the valley, and the peacocks crowing arrogantly at everyone. I loved this place; two nights are an absolute minimum. *Best visited between December and May.*

Rooms: 30: 6 doubles, 24 twins, all with en suite shower.
Price: R140 – R215 pp sharing. Single supplement about 50%.
Meals: Full breakfast included. Lunch by arrangement R25 – R40. Dinner R50 for as much as you want.
Directions: Faxed or emailed on booking.

Gauteng

Melrose Place Guest Lodge

Sue Truter

12a North St, Melrose, 2196
Tel: 011-442-5231 Fax: 011-880-2371
Email: suetruter@global.co.za Web: www.melroseplace.co.za
Cell: 083-457-4021

Once ensconced behind the electric gates at Melrose you have entered an Eden-in-the-city. The verandah overlooks a large flower garden and enormous swimming pool, all shaded by trees. Eight new rooms don't crowd it at all. It is such a pleasant environment that you may find yourself shelving projected tasks for a day's lounging about. My room was a suite attached to the main house, with mounted TV, huge bed (built up with cushions and pillows), a big bathroom and double doors onto the garden. The high levels of luxury in all the rooms are not reflected in the rates. Sue is the sweetest of hostesses, quick to smiles and reacting sensitively to the mood and wishes of each guest. On the night I stayed we had a braai with an amazing array of meat dishes and salads which appeared from nowhere, and Sue's team will cook dinner for anyone who wants it every evening. Her aim is to maximise the number of happy campers staying. This is her home after all, complete with kids, dachshund and a parrot in its forties. While guest contentment is running at 100 per cent it's difficult to see what else she can do. *Laundry provided on request. Nearby: Wanderers cricket ground, Rosebank and Sandton shopping precincts and many restaurants. Airport transfers arranged by Sue.*

Rooms: 14: all en suite (1 bath only, 4 bath and shower, 9 shower only); includes two cottages.
Price: R250 – R300 pp sharing. Singles R400 – R450.
Meals: Full breakfast included. Lunches or dinners by arrangement: R65.
Directions: Ask for a map when booking. Or a map on the web site.

Map Number 11

Iketleng in the Gardens

Sheila Weinberg

12 Plantation Road, Gardens
Tel: 011-728-3030 Fax: 011-728-3030
Email: sheilaw@sn.apc.org Web: www.iketleng.co.za
Cell: 082-855-8493

Sheila's principled life-time support of the South African liberation movement saw her detained without trial in 1964. Today she is a member of the Gauteng Provincial Legislature but I'll let her tell her own story, which is fascinating and an excellent reason to stay in her B&B. And it is a B&B in the proper sense, i.e. you share the house with Sheila. The flourishing garden, boasting some exotic plants including a tall aloe Barbarae, attracts much bird life and you can sit out on the patio for breakfast. The house is simply furnished and bedrooms have wooden floors, heaters, showers with good pressure and tiled floors. There are books and CDs, TV and brochures on the state of the New South Africa in the open-plan sitting room. I recommend Iketleng (which means 'let's enjoy ourselves' in Sotho) not for high luxury (it is very comfortable though), but for a fascinating perspective on the old and new South Africas and for Sheila's sense of fun. Footwear is optional in the house. Roger, a guest, was wearing socks. Sheila goes barefoot. I chose shoes.

Rooms: 5: 4 doubles, 1 single; all with en/s bathrooms, 2 with baths, 3 with showers.
Price: R220 – R280 pp sharing. Singles R270 – R330.
Meals: Full breakfast included. 200 metres to the 4 nearest restaurants!
Directions: Ask when booking.

Liz's at Lancaster

Liz Delmont

79 Lancaster Ave, Craighall Park, 2196
Tel: 011-442-8083 Fax: 011-880-5969
Email: lizdel@megaweb.co.za Web: www.lizatlancaster.co.za
Cell: 083-229-4223

Liz's place on its own is a lovely B&B (more on that later), but throw in Liz as well and you get something special. In my limited experience she is an anomaly among South Africans, having no great interest in rugby, football or cricket, and this despite being surrounded by a sports-mad family. Liz teaches art history and post-graduate tourism development at Witwatersrand University, and is a fascinating person to speak to about South Africa both past and future and about Joburg. She will point you in all the right directions for a genuine, heartfelt and hard-to-come-by insight into her home city. But guests at Liz's also have plenty of space in which to do their own thing. The big comfy rooms are either side of the main house, and both have their own entrances and parking spaces – one also has a kitchen and sitting room. Each opens up onto a private patio, where breakfast is generally served, with potted plants climbing up the walls and plenty of shade. Between the two is a rose-filled garden, while at the front of the house is yet more green space (the garden has grown since the photo was taken) around the pool. Finally, a mention for the friendly staff, who have a stake in the venture.

Rooms: 2 double rooms with en suite shower and bath, one with kitchen and sitting room too.
Price: R280 – R380 pp sharing. Singles R420 – R560
Meals: Full breakfast included. Dinners on request but very close to Parkhurst and many restaurants.
Directions: Jan Smuts Ave runs down the middle of the city and Lancaster Ave is off it. Directions on web site.

North West Province

Madikwe Bush House

Di Casey
Madikwe Game Reserve
Tel: 011-708-1709 Fax: 011-708-1980
Email: reservations@madikwehouse.co.za
Web: www.madikwehouse.co.za Cell: 083-231-7409

The name says it like it is. This is not a bush lodge or camp, but a house that happens to be in the bush, to wit a magnificent converted 1920s farmhouse next to a waterhole in Madikwe game reserve. With its huge garden and creature comforts (big sofas, cosy pub, there is even a TV "for sporting emergencies"), it is unashamedly the soft option. There are deep beds with crisp sheets (heaters in winter, aircon in summer) to retire to at night, but you will still spend much of your time either out in the bush or on the lawn, sipping a cold one. The reserve's 75,000 hectares, once cattle stations, were returned to mother nature in 1990, when over 8,000 animals were transplanted here from all over the world (numbers have since multiplied for most species) including all the big-five crowd-pleasers (elephants, rhinos and the like) and rarer beasts such as African wild dogs. Game drives yield frequent sightings. My favourite spot was the rock pool just inside the fence from the waterhole, but there are lots to choose from. Dinners are a real treat, whether in the boma under the reserve's only baobab tree or at the long, sociable dining-room table. All in all, the Bush House is an intimate, relaxed, child-friendly, malaria-free, great-value, all-weather, absolute gem of a place!

Rooms: 6: 2 doubles and 4 twins; all with en suite shower/bath.
Price: Fully inclusive: from R1095 per person.
Meals: Full breakfast, dinner, brunch, high tea, game drives included. Drinks are extra.
Directions: Western side of the Madikwe Game Reserve. N4 from Pretoria to Zeerust. It's 91 km north of there on the R49.

Mosetlha Bush Camp

Chris and June Lucas
Madikwe Game Reserve
Tel: 011-444-9345 Fax: 011-802-6222
Email: info@thebushcamp.com Web: www.thebushcamp.com
Cell: 083-653-9869

Mosetlha puts the wild into wilderness; no doors or glass here as they would hinder the feel and dust of Africa permeating your very core; no electric fences surround the camp as there is no electricity; no worries either as you leave them at the gate. Facilities are basic but real; guests draw their own hot water from a donkey-boiler before proceeding to the shower. The wooden huts are comfortable but used only for sleeping – you are here for the wilderness experience of the outdoors. Chris's passion for conservation and his environment shines through and is contagious (which reminds me to say that the area is malaria-free). His guests depart much the wiser, not only because of the game drives, but also because of the superb guided wilderness walks. Yes, the Madikwe Game Reserve (70,000 hectares) has the so-called 'Big Five' but a game lodge worth its salt (such as this) will fire your imagination about the whole food chain. Even the camp itself is an education – all sorts of birds, small mammals and antelopes venture in. Come for a genuine and memorable bush experience.

Rooms: 8 twins sharing 3 shower / toilet complexes.
Price: All-inclusive from R695 per person. Drinks extra.
Meals: All meals and refreshments included.
Directions: Detailed written directions supplied on request.

Limpopo Province

The Coach House

Guy Matthews

Old Coach Rd, Agatha, near Tzaneen, 0850
Tel: 015-306-8000 reservations: 015-306-8027 Fax: 015-306-8008
Email: coachhouse@mweb.co.za Web: www.coachhouse.co.za
Cell: 083-627-9999

The Coach House *is* a hotel, but it is a rare achievement in the genre to retain such a friendly and personal atmosphere; this is down to a dynamic Guy Matthews and his attentive team. You are encouraged to slow down, switch off, breathe in the air and maybe take a snooze on your own patio. The setting is spectacular, although the Drakensberg hid coyly behind the mist when I stayed. The food is also delicious and comes mostly from the surrounding farms. There is a floodlit croquet lawn (if you can muster the energy), a keyhole-shaped pool, a new spa with heated pool number two, a substantial gym and a variety of treatment rooms. You can also go hiking in the grounds (560 hectares, mostly dedicated to macadamia and pecan nut plantations), or sample the joys of the little nougat factory, the snooker room with views of the lowveld, the sitting room with roaring fires, and the oldest (109 years!) money jukebox in the world. Since the first edition people have continued to speak highly of the Coach House and it deserves its excellent reputation. *No children under 14. Kruger National Park is 100 km away. Close to the Coach House: Rooikat Forest Trail, Debegeni waterfalls, and Tzaneen and Ebenezer dams for fishing.*

Rooms: 41 rooms, all with en suite bathrooms.
Price: From R525 – R925 pp sharing including breakfast. Single room R680 – R900 including breakfast.
Meals: All meals available in the restaurant. Casual breakfasts: R80 – R100. 3-course set-menu dinners in the restaurant: R160 – R200 (wine extra).
Directions: Ask when booking.

Garonga Safari Camp

Bernardo Smith
Gravelotte
Tel: Res: 011-537-4620 Camp:082-440-3522
Fax: Res: 011-447-0993 Camp:082-806-2905
Email: reservations@garonga.com Web: www.garonga.com

Garonga is as close to Heaven as most of us ever get. Bernardo has succeeded in creating a luxurious, yet completely relaxed, North African oasis in the middle of the South African bush: terracotta colours, thick earthen walls, cushions on low beds and billowing white fabrics. The pace is slow and unpressurised, the perfect relaxed environment for honeymooners, couples celebrating anniversaries – or for just about anyone who needs to make it up to someone else. Game drives are always available, but you may prefer to lie in under the high, white-tented canopy of your amazing room, dreaming of the candlelit bath taken under the stars on the previous evening with a bottle of wine; or of the sensational food you have enjoyed and hope still to enjoy. Alternately you can choose a more solitary, more exotic night's sleep twenty minutes from camp on a platform high above the water. Still stressed? Then return to Garonga and fall asleep in one of the hammocks or be pampered by the resident aromatherapist while gazing languidly over the nearby waterhole. Probably the most romantic place to stay in this book.

Rooms: 7 : 6 rooms with indoor and outdoor shower; 1 bush suite with bath, shower and outdoor shower and air-conditioning.
Price: Winter: R1375 pp sharing. Summer R2375 – R3050 pp sharing.
Meals: All inclusive (except for the more expensive wines).
Directions: Directions will be given to you when you book.

Map Number 16

Tshukudu Game Lodge

Lolly and Ala Sussens

Hoedspruit, 1380
Tel: 015-793-2476 Fax: 015-793-2078
Email: tshukudu@iafrica.com Web: www.tshukudulodge.co.za
Cell: 083-626-4916

"You snooze, you lose," goes up the cry on Tshukudu's unique morning walking safari. It is just as well to listen to the ranger's advice unless you want the accompanying lion leaping onto your back or a young (but big!) elephant knocking you over. There is true adventure here and not only for the children for whom Tshukudu is paradise. This is an active reserve where orphaned animals are reared and re-introduced to the wild, and it is possible to encounter animals that have made the successful transition. Guests are encouraged to share in the process, meeting the animals close up and walking through the bush with them. There are two game drives a day too, but plenty of opportunity to relax at the pool or the thatched bar. Dinner is a group affair, usually in the circular reed boma under the stars, where only the delicious buffet interrupts excited chatter. There are many game lodges in the Kruger area, but precious few are family-built, -owned and –managed. A warm, involving and edifying experience. Great for kids.

Rooms: 13: all doubles or twins with shower en suite.
Price: From R1200 – R1400 pp sharing, from R1050 – R1250 single (children under 12 are half price). Includes all meals, game drives and walks.
Meals: All meals are included, but not drinks.
Directions: R40 north from Nelspruit . 4 km north from Hoedspruit turn right at the Tshukudu sign – 6 km down dirt road.

Gomo Gomo Game Lodge

Van Zyl Manktelow & Ryan Ashton
Timbavati Game Reserve
Tel: 013-752-3954 (reservations) Fax: 013-752-3002 (reservations)
Email: gomo@netactive.co.za Web: www.gomogomo.co.za
Cell: 082-454-2571

When Simon visited Gomo Gomo two years ago, he edged heroically past four male lions, sighted wart hogs, elephant and zebra, and all before he had been welcomed into camp. On arriving this time round, I learnt that one of the gardeners had just slain a spitting cobra with a slingshot and a leopard had killed an impala in camp. This bush is not for taming! Electricity has been added, but fans and bedside lamps complement, rather than compromise, the bush atmosphere. You sleep in rondavels or safari tents (I prefer the latter), some of which are river facing and have private decks. A day in camp usually contains morning and evening game drives and a bush walk before guests gather for dinner in the boma and sit round a fire in as much of a circle as numbers allow. Want to or not, you will find yourself telling big-game stories (or at least big stories about game). The camp sits right by the Nhlaralumi River (swimming is a mite hazardous – fewer crocs and hippos in the pool) and the sounds of the night will stay with you (in a good way) for a long time. To top it all, managers Rudi and Ancabé are an impressively enthusiastic couple, a vital element, which makes the camp stand taller than others.

Rooms: 8: 5 brick and thatch rondavels: 3 with 2 bedrooms, 4 with bathroom with shower; 1 with bath; 3 luxury safari tents all with en/s shower.
Price: R700 – R1250 pp sharing. Single supplement R350.
Meals: Full breakfast, lunch and dinner, game drives included. Extras are your bar bill and your curio purchases.
Directions: From Hoedspruit take the R40 south for km. Go left at Eastgate Airport sign. Follow to the gate – signed to Gomo Gomo in the park.

Umlani Bushcamp

Marco Schiess

Timbavati Nature Reserve
Tel: 012-346-4028 Fax: 012-346-4023
Email: umlani@mweb.co.za Web: www.umlani.com
Cell: 083-468-2041

Rhino-tracking on foot; a rather exciting experience with a couple of bull elephants; sun-downers as the bush settles for the night.... This is what safaris are supposed to be about, and Umlani delivers. The camp is set on a gentle slope above a dry river course (wet in spring) and no fence separates you from the Timbavati Nature Reserve's more feral inhabitants – you do not leave your hut at night to investigate snuffling noises! You sleep in comfortable reed-walled rondavels with thatched roofs (no bricks here) and no electricity, and you shower *au naturel*, in complete privacy, looking out over the greenery. Marco and his wife Marie ran the camp by themselves for a decade until the demands of a young family compelled them to find some help in the form of Alan and Mandy, two of the most delightful managers you could hope to find. After the evening game drive everyone sits out on the deck by the bar, mulling over what's just been seen before sitting down for dinner and mulling over the affairs of the world. Thoughtful hosts and knowledgeable rangers provide the charming, human face of a full-on bush experience. Civilisation in the midst of the wild.

Rooms: 8: 7 doubles, 1 sleeps 4; all with en/s outside showers.
Price: From R1350 – R1650 pp sharing. Singles R1500 – R1870.
Meals: All meals, drinks and 2-3 game activities included.
Directions: You will get a map when you book.

Tangala Safari Camp

Eugene Potgieter
Thornybush Nature Reserve
Tel: Res:015-793-0321 (h): 083-288-2555
Fax: Res:015-793-0321 (h): 015-793-0543
Email: reservations@tangala.co.za Web: www.tangala.co.za

"Just nip around the rhino – he's somewhere up ahead – and we'll see you back at the lodge in a few minutes." Such was my introduction to Tangala as I drove past the other guests on their evening game drive. Situated in the middle of the Thornybush Game Reserve, the camp offers a true bush experience and Eugene is its king. A cross between Errol Flynn and David Attenborough, he's a mine of swash-buckling wisdom who knows pretty much every darn thing about the wild. He spent years working for the Department of Nature Conservation before turning the Potgieter family holiday home into a safari camp. There is a kind of rugged luxury here. No wooden masks adorn the walls, but sherry greets your evening return and drums call you to eat. There is no electricity to remind you of home, but the thatched huts provide ample delights; voluminous mozzie nets, hurricane lamps, thick towels and a choir of cicadas combine to lull you to sleep. Game viewing is generally excellent – I was lucky enough to see all the 'Big 5' inside 24 hours – and not necessarily that far away. Two days before my arrival, guests had watched a lion take down a wildebeest right opposite the bar. All is, of course, entirely safe, but half the fun is to believe otherwise.

Rooms: 5: 4 twins, 1 double (with 2 extra beds); 4 with en/s shower, 1 with en/s bath.
Price: R980 – R1320 pp sharing.
Meals: Brunch, tea, 3-course supper, game drive snacks and 2 game drives included.
Directions: Map can be faxed or emailed when you book.

Pezulu Tree House Lodge

Gilly and West Mathewson
PO Box 795, Hoedspruit, 1380
Tel: 015-793-2724
Fax: 015-793-2253
Email: pezlodge@mweb.co.za
Web: www.pezulu.co.za
Cell: 083-376-3048

The sorry victim of a treehouse-free childhood, I was intrigued by the concept of Pezulu – six different reed-and-thatch constructions spread among the trees surrounding the central building, which is itself entwined around a large amarula. They are all hidden from view behind branch and leaf, and many have bits of tree growing up through the floor to provide the most natural of towel rails, stools and loo paper holders. The 'houses' are named after the trees in which they sit: 'False Thorn' has a magnificent shower with views over the Thornybush Reserve – be prepared for inquisitive giraffe; while 'Huilboerboom' is a honeymoon suite set eight metres above ground (privacy even from the giraffe). Gilly's husband West conjured Pezulu out of the Guernsey Conservancy on the edge of the Kruger Park. There are no predators in this area, only plains game, so you and the buck can wander around the property in perfect safety. Activities on offer include the usual two game drives a day and/ or guided hikes. They can also arrange microlight flights and visits to rehabilitation centres and the white lion breeding project... assuming they can persuade you down from the trees.

Rooms: 6: 1 family unit (1 double and 1 twin), 5 doubles; 1 with en/s shower; 2 with separate bath; 3 with separate shower.
Price: All-inclusive rate: R1150 – R1380 pp sharing. R1300 – R1560 for singles.
Meals: Fully inclusive of all meals, game activities, microlight flights, guided day trips to Kruger and tours of the Panoramic Route. No drinks included.
Directions: Ask when booking.

Mpumalanga

Rissington Inn

Chris Harvie
PO Box 650, Hazyview, 1242
Tel: 013-737-7700 Fax: 013-737-7112
Email: rissington@mweb.co.za Web: www.rissington.co.za

Informality and relaxation dictate at the Rissington Inn; you feel this even as you mount the broad steps to the verandah for the first time. Sun-lounging guests dazily contemplate the flower gardens full of frangipani; the swimming pool is a rectangle of cool aquamarine; the hazy valley shimmers beyond. In the evenings gourmet candlelit dinners are served by friendly staff and residents get first stab at the verandah tables. These meals are incredible value. We have eaten with Chris on four separate occasions and never been disappointed, despite much creativity and daring in the dishes. High ceilings put the lid on well-designed themed rooms. The one I had was enormous with a Victorian bathroom and its own sitting area. But Rissington isn't the sort of place where you feel like hiding away or watching TV. Owner/mover/shaker Chris actually seems to LIKE seeing his guests doing what they want, dressed how they feel and making friends. When you arrive there is usually a gaggle of guests lined up at his wooden bar and you could easily mistake them for Chris's personal friends. They probably only arrived a few minutes before you. *Hazyview sits at the portals of the Kruger National Park.*

Rooms: 10: 8 doubles and 2 twins, all with en/s bathrooms, 6 with bath and shower, 4 with bath.
Price: R210 – R390 pp sharing. Single supplement + 50%.
Meals: Full breakfast included and served till noon. Lunch approx. R30 and dinner à la carte approx R80 – R100.
Directions: 2 km south of Hazyview on R40 White River Numbi Gate (KNP) Rd. On right coming from main Hazyview 4-way stop – see signs for Rissington and Kiaat Park.

Map Number 16

Notten's Bush Camp

Bambi and Gilly Notten
(Sabi Sand Game Reserve), Hazyview, 1242
Tel: 013-735-5105 Fax: 013-735-5970
Email: nottens@iafrica.com Web: www.nottens.com

You would have to arrive at Notten's in the mother of all moods to ignore the palpable friendliness which washes over you like a cool breeze. Few camps now are owner-run and you really can sense the difference. The Nottens have kept the camp small – only twelve guests stay at any one time – and they treat all who visit as friends. You feel instantly at home on the main verandah with its photos, sculptures and camaraderie. The family manage the trick of providing a true bush experience without compromising on comfort, and this helps explain why so many return year after year. Game drives traverse territory rich in wildlife, and sightings are excitedly discussed under the stars in the boma. (Romantics rest assured: electricity has not been added since the first edition, although solar-powered fans cool your summer slumbers). Chalets tend happily towards the classical with white linen, dark woods and private decks. And if it all gets too exciting, head for the pool and soak up the almost unreal (surreal?) African tableau of game, plain and waterhole that spreads before you. Notten's is a camp that continues to get a nod of approval from those who know their safaris, and once again we'd like to give it a special nod of our own.

Rooms: 5: 3 doubles, 1 twin and 1 family room all with en/s showers – 2 have outdoor showers as well.
Price: R1700 – R2250 pp sharing. Single supplement 50%.
Meals: All meals are included in the price (except bar drinks).
Directions: Ask when booking.

Lion Sands Private Game Reserve

Robert More
Sabi Sands
Tel: 013-735-5000 Fax: 013-735-5330
Email: res@lionsands.com Web: www.lionsands.com

Set in 3,700 thrilling hectares in the Sabi Sand Game Reserve, Lion Sands is a new, family-run operation that provides a luxurious safari experience without ever forgetting to be friendly, welcoming and enormous fun. Owned by the same family since 1932, it's the only property in the reserve with substantial access to the Sabie River and you can sit by room or pool and applaud the wildlife show that the river stages day and night. There are two camps at present, the more informal River Lodge and the more exclusive South Camp. Both possess an opulence which is established from your first steps into River Lodge, and continues throughout the purple-themed dining room and soaring thatched bar area – or the smaller versions at South Camp. Evening meals happen in one of myriad locations: dining room, boma, bush, river-bed braai or privately and romantically overlooking the river bed. Bedrooms are rondavels with river-facing extensions, supremely comfortable mattresses and most else that the heart can desire. And to top it all off, they have some superb game viewing. Mine started early as a young lioness chased my car, and at dawn the next day we saw a leopard within a minute of leaving camp. A wonderful place with tremendous staff and atmosphere – get there soon.

Rooms: 20: River Lodge, 14 rooms; South Lodge, 6 rooms. All are convertible twin/doubles with en/s bath, shower and outdoor shower.
Price: River Lodge, low season: from R2350; high season: from R3185. South Camp, low season: from R2750; high season: from R3640. Single supplement + 35%.
Meals: All meals and 2 game drives and drinks on game drives included. Other drinks at meal times excluded.
Directions: Map can be faxed. From Hazyview follow signs to Kruger Gate. Turn left at Lion Sands sign off and follow signs to River Lodge or South Camp.

Idube Private Game Reserve

Sally Kernick
Sabi Sand Game Reserve
Tel: 011-888-3713 Fax: 011-888-2181
Email: info@idube.com Web: www.idube.com

There are few establishments where the staff seem to have as much fun working together as at Idube. Be they guides, trackers, managers or chefs, the Idube crew exude a delightful sense of goodwill to each other and to all mankind. And it's not difficult to see why. Warthog roam through the camp, elephants pass nearby; there is space and greenery, beauty and beast. The land was bought in 1983 by Louis and Marilyn Marais and Louis sensibly built the swimming pool before designing and constructing the rest of the camp himself. Guests sleep in chalets dotted around the sloping grounds, while the thatched seating and dining areas look out over the Sabi-Sand Game Reserve. A rope bridge over the river bed takes you to a hide where you can admire the Shadulu dam and its regulars without being admired yourself. Two game drives per day plus guided walks give you the chance to see what's happening elsewhere in the reserve and tracker Titus amazed us with his ability to read bent grasses and droppings. We took time out for sundowners by a dam, accompanied by a bull elephant and a bull hippo. There was much posturing and manliness, not least from me, before a return to camp for dinner and conviviality under the stars.

Rooms: 10: 2 doubles, 8 twins. All with en/s bathrooms and outdoor showers.
Price: Winter (May to end Sept) R1450 – R1750 pp sharing. Summer (October to end April) R2250 – R2500. Single supplement +35%.
Meals: All 3 meals plus morning and evening drives and a guided walk included. Drinks and tranfers extra.
Directions: 34.4 km from Hazyview along R536 towards Kruger Gate. Follow signs off to the left. 19.5.km along a dirt road.

Kavinga Guest House

Stuart and Ros Hulley-Miller
R37 Nelspruit/Sabie Rd, Nelspruit, 1200
Tel: 013-755-3193 Fax: 013-755-3161
Email: kavinga@mpu.co.za
Cell: 083-625-7162

Thick orchards of avocados buffer Kavinga farmhouse and its green lake of lawn from the outside world. Ros assembles a country breakfast on the stone-tiled verandah, which is latticed with rare jade vine and camouflaged by plants and flowers. If you are like the majority of the Hulley-Millers' guests you will spend a good deal of time there, lying on wicker furniture and deck chairs or flopping indolently in the pool while Ros dispenses indispensable drinks. Brightly-coloured bedrooms dotted around the grounds are furnished antiquely, but pander to the twenty-first century with satellite TV, bar fridges and sumptuous bathrooms (with both shower and free-standing bath). The family unit has its own sitting room with a sofa bed to unravel for extra bodies. French windows open onto small covered patios with broad views over the Lowveld. I think it was Walt Disney's Baloo the Bear who said: 'Float downstream, fall apart in my backyard'.... *Just 45 km to the Kruger National Park.*

Rooms: 5: 3 twins, 1 double and 1 family unit with 1 double and 1 twin – all with en suite baths and showers.
Price: R195 – R235 pp sharing. Singles R245 – R285.
Meals: Full breakfast included. Dinner by arrangement: R65 for 3 courses.
Directions: 14.5 km north from Nelspruit on R37 towards Sabie. Sign to right.

The Artists' Café and Guest House

Brenda Tod
Hendriksdal Sdg., district Sabie, 1260
Tel: 013-764-2309 Fax: 013-764-2309
Email: artscafe@mweb.co.za
Cell: 082-9577-477

The Artists' Café, once a station master's house, is now an inspired restaurant and art gallery – all the paintings, sculptures and carvings in the bar area are by Lowveld artists and for sale. To get to your room you walk along the railway line – in the dark you are given a paraffin lamp – through pine trees, over lawns, past herb and flower gardens. The 'Hendriksdal' railway sign welcomes you to the two Waiting Rooms, the Station Master's Office and the Ticket Office, now transmogrified into charming, white-walled bedrooms. "There's nothing frilly," says Brenda happily. Food is fresh, rural Italian (predominantly Tuscan) in style, cooked by Brenda and served by a lively array of helpers. The railway is occasionally still used which only adds to the charm, although the odd shunt in the early morning by a timber train can wake light sleepers. Unpretentious, unique and very friendly. *Award-winning wine list.*

Rooms: 4 rooms, all with en suite bathrooms, 2 with baths, 2 with showers.
Price: For a single night's stay: R205 – R245 pp sharing, R245 – R295 for singles. For 2 nights or more: R185 pp sharing, R225 single.
Meals: Full breakfast included. Lunch and dinner available in à la carte restaurant.
Directions: On the R37 between Nelspruit and Sabie, but ask when you book for more detail!

Hops Hollow Country House

Theo and Sarie de Beer
PO Box 430, Lydenburg, 1120
Tel: 013-235-2275 or 083-627-6940 Fax: 083-627-6940
Email: hops@intekom.co.za
Cell: 083-281-7113

The highest brewery in South Africa, Hops Hollow combines the warmest of welcomes with home-made beers, scrumptious meals and a picturesque setting. There is something rather Scottish about the scenery surrounding this guest-house high on the Long Tom Pass, with its mountains, mist and crisp air. The area has many Boer War and gold-rush connections and Theo will tell you about both historical and natural wonders. Following a Damascene conversion one moonlit night he gave up clerical work for life in conservation and has never looked back. When not at his day job with the Mpumalanga Parks Board he's a proper microbrewer (supply your own 'De Beer' pun – Theo suggests "brewing de Beer on de mountain") and loves showing guests around his brewery. A rather baronial pub with vast columns made from old railway sleepers should be complete by late 2002. Sarie, meanwhile, is the force behind the guest house whose bedrooms have thick duvets and large cushions and, in some cases, views best appreciated from the pillow. She is also a wonderful cook (lots of beer in the recipes) and I defy you to leave Hops Hollow with your belt on the same notch. This small, twin-pronged business is a delight, for ale-lovers and otherwise.

Rooms: 3: all twin/doubles with en/s showers.
Price: R230 – R275 pp sharing. Singles R250 – R300.
Meals: Full breakfast included. Dinner by prior arrangement. 3 courses – price varies. Bigger meals in winter.
Directions: On R37 between Sabie and Lydenburg, opposite milestone 22.2 on the Long Tom Pass (distance from Lydenburg).

Swaziland

Phophonyane Lodge

Lungile de Vletter

PO Box 199, Pigg's Peak
Tel: +268-437-1429 Fax: +268-437-1319
Email: lungile@africaonline.co.sz Web: www.phophonyane.co.sz
Cell: +268-604-2802

A South African visa is enough to see you popping over the border into the Kingdom of Swaziland and immersing yourself in 500 hectares of pristine nature. Phophonyane Lodge is perched high on a valleyside in thick indigenous forest with the constant background music of a thousand birds (230 species) and the rushing white water of the Phophonyane River cascading down the kloof below (waterfall-viewing walks are a must). You move between the main lodge and the various tents and cottages on cobbles and wooden walkways, past murals and rough wood sculptures, natural materials blending easily into the landscape. Some of the cottages have sitting rooms, private gardens, narrow wooden staircases up to bedrooms and balconies, big showers, kitchens et al. The safari tents with their private decks are simpler but more romantic. You are lost in the trees and I stayed in one of the two right down by the rushing water's edge, the best sleeping draught imaginable. The reserve is criss-crossed with hiking paths leading to natural rock pools for swimming, and guests congregate at the bar in the evenings to watch the sun go down. Family-owned and run, Phophonyane is perfect for outdoorsy nature lovers. *4x4 drives to mountains and Bushman paintings available.*

Rooms: 4 cottages (3 sleep 5, 1 sleeps 2); 2 with shower, 1 with b, 1 with b and sh. 5 tents (4 sleep 3, 1 sleeps 2); 1 has en/s sh, the others nearby private bathroom.
Price: R203 – R425 pp sharing. Singles R268 – R615. Continental breakfast R25, English breakfast R35.
Meals: Each unit is self-catering, except some tents. A la carte restaurant available and picnic lunches can be prepared.
Directions: 14 km north of Pigg's Peak Town or 35 km from Jeppe's Reef border post to sign posts then +/- 4 km of dirt road following the signs to the entrance.

Index

Index by town name

Index

Index by house name

THE GREENWOOD GUIDE TO
AUSTRALIA AND
NEW ZEALAND

Special Hand-Picked Accommodation

The second in the Greenwood Guides series offers you the chance to follow our many footsteps across both these countries.

We have chosen only the friendliest B&Bs, farms, lodges, wilderness camps and small hotels covering the whole of Australia and New Zealand...

...and much too that does not fit easily into any category, such as an overnight stay in Sydney Zoo, a desert camel safari, boat charters for the Whitsunday Islands, a lighthouse and an old jail.

ALSO... The first edition of the Greenwood Guide to Canada is due for publication in spring 2003. For information or to order any of our books see our website at www.greenwoodguides.com or email us at editor@greenwoodguides.com.

THE GREENWOOD GUIDE TO
AUSTRALIA &
NEW ZEALAND

special hand-picked
accommodation

Researched and written by
Simon and Fiona Greenwood and Tom Bell